CORYDON
BELL

# SHADOW PLAYS
## AND HOW TO PRODUCE THEM

Books by

WINIFRED H. MILLS

and

LOUISE M. DUNN

*"Marionettes, Masks and Shadows"*

*"Shadow Plays and How to Produce Them"*

Behind the screen during performance of "The Carnival of the Animals" at the Cleveland Museum of Art

# SHADOW PLAYS

## AND HOW TO PRODUCE THEM

*by*

WINIFRED H. MILLS

*Assistant Professor of Art, Louisiana State University*

*&*

LOUISE M. DUNN

*Associate Curator of Education, The Cleveland Museum of Art*

ILLUSTRATED BY CORYDON BELL

DOUBLEDAY, DORAN & CO., INC., NEW YORK

1938

PRINTED AT THE *Country Life Press*, GARDEN CITY, N. Y., U. S. A.



CL



FIRST EDITION

*To the great Shadow Makers*
*who through imagination and skill*
*have been able to reveal*
*the subtle power and beauty*
*of the Shadow World.*

## CONTENTS

CONTENTS

## PART II: SHADOW PLAYS WITH MUSIC



## PART III: HUMAN SHADOW PLAYS

# ILLUSTRATIONS

## Diagrams



## Photographs

## ILLUSTRATIONS

ILLUSTRATIONS

## ILLUSTRATIONS

# INTRODUCTION

## The Earliest Shadow Plays and Their Present-Day Influence

# INTRODUCTION

## The Earliest Shadow Plays and Their Present-Day Influence

SHADOWS HAVE always had a strange fascination for mankind. They are mysterious, illusive and often disquieting, and it is easy to understand how they played upon the imagination of primitive people, provoking fear and superstition. What could be more baffling than a man's own shadow that followed him everywhere, that he could not escape except in utter darkness? Sometimes these shadows seemed ominous, at other times sacred. His shadow was a part of him, perhaps his soul, he must guard it as he would his life. Throughout the ages many primitive people have never entirely lost this regard for shadows. Even today travelers among primitive people in many far-scattered lands have come upon startling evidence of this fear of shadows, especially among the tribes of central and southern Africa and among the Australian Bushmen and the North American Indians. For example, the savages of Wetar, a tribe of West Africa, jealously guard their shadows in fear of bad luck, and never allow anyone to step upon them. For the same reason the Bushman of Australia will never allow his shadow to fall on dead game.

Certain Malay tribes will not permit their shadow

to fall into the hole that is being dug for the center pole of a new house, lest sickness and death follow. In southeastern Europe there are similar superstitions concerning shadows. For instance, in parts of Roumania, we are told, there are people who believe, as did the ancient Greeks, that if the measure of a strong man's shadow is buried in the foundations of a new building that man's strength will pass into it.

In place of a superstitious fear of shadows, there came eventually the discovery that man could make and control a shadow world of his own. It is thought that this idea developed when the people saw the silhouettes of the priests, performing holy rites, fall on the sides of the sacred tent.

Probably China can claim the honor of originating the shadow play as we know it today. There is an old legend of an emperor who became so exasperated with his two court fools that he ordered their heads cut off. No sooner was this done than the irascible emperor found life very dull without their antics. Calling his grand vizier, he ordered him to bring the fools back to life. Of course the vizier was almost at his wit's end. He knew he would lose his own head if he could not fulfill the royal command. As he was trying desperately to think of a way out of his difficulty, he happened upon a fisherman carrying two great fish. The vizier evidently knew something of the possibilities of dried fish skin, and at once he had an inspiration. He bought the fish and set about his task of preparing the skins. Finally he managed to cut out two figures that very cleverly suggested the court jesters. With similar skill and cleverness he was able to show the tyrannical emperor his fools, this time as shadow figures performing their antics against a lighted screen. These shadow actors entertained the emperor even more than the living jesters.

From China the shadow theater passed to many Oriental countries, to Bali, Java, Japan, Persia and Turkey, to take on new forms and express different cultural ideas.

The earliest authentic historical dates and circumstances of the Chinese shadow play fall during the reign of the Emperor Wu Ti, sixth emperor of the Han dynasty, who reigned between 157–87 B.C. And what a fascinating story it is! This poet emperor began his reign when he was but sixteen years old. Among the many beautiful young women of his court his favorite was Li Fujen. When she died he was unconsolable. Famous wizards were sent for, in the hope that they might be able to bring back from the land of shades the spirit of the beloved Li Fujen.

Her shadow, when it appeared, was so realistic that the visit was repeated night after night for the consolation of the bereaved emperor, who bestowed upon the magician the title of "master of perfection." From this time on it became a common practice to recall the "shadows of the souls of the dead" as an accompaniment to religious rites.

Beyond a doubt shadow figures and shadow screens were well known to the Chinese magicians at least a hundred years before the birth of Christ. Following their early royal recognition, shadow plays came to have an important part in the development of the Chinese theater.

## SHADOW PLAYS

Storytellers went from village to village telling their tales through shadow figures. The designing and making of shadow figures and scenery, as well as their manipulation, gradually became an exacting art. The skins of pigs, goats, donkeys, water buffalo and certain fish were prepared with great care to make them suitable and enduring. The figures were exquisitely designed. Much ingenuity went into the articulating of the joints of these shadow figures, so that they might be able to make the most subtle movements and gestures. With slender thongs of skin and threads of silk the joints were secured. As a last bit of perfection these figures were pierced and incised in beautiful designs and then exquisitely colored with transparent dyes. When the figures were complete in every detail, they were attached at the neck and hands to slender rods of wood, bamboo, bone or ivory. By means of these rods, which extended below the shadow figures, the puppeteers were able to control and manipulate them.

Certain families of artists gave all their time to the making of shadow figures and scenery; and to the presenting of shadow plays for all sorts of occasions to people of widely different interests and tastes. As this was a means of livelihood and required a long and exacting apprenticeship, it was quite natural that children and grandchildren followed the calling of their family. Thus a tradition developed in the practice of this unusual art. Even today, after more than twenty centuries, it is still possible in certain districts of China to find a few traveling companies of shadow players. They no longer know when their ancestors

Behind the screen with the Red Gate Shadow Players

Scene from a Chinese shadow play given by the Red Gate Shadow Players

Properties for a Chinese shadow play

took up the "shadows" as a means of a livelihood.

Travelers who have been privileged to see these shadow performances in China have marveled at the amazing illusions these artists are able to create, and have sometimes acquired shadow figures to bring back to their friends in Europe and America. Some of these figures have found their way into museum collections in France, Germany, Holland, England and America. In the United States they are to be found in several museums as well as private collections. The late Professor Berthold Laufer brought together an outstanding collection for the Field Museum of Chicago and wrote an interesting handbook, in which much is to be learned of "Oriental theatricals."

Another fine collection of Chinese shadow figures in our country is in the Brooklyn Museum. The Cleveland Museum of Art has some excellent examples in its lending collection for schools and libraries. This has become very practical and inspiring material for the students who wish to create modern shadow figures for modern shadow plays.

While in no other country have the shadow figures attained the high degree of perfection that they have attained in China, yet the shadow figures from the islands of Java and Bali have much in common with those of China, and possibly rank second in beauty. They are made in much the same way and usually from skins, but they differ from the Chinese shadow figures in their design. They have an amazing exaggeration of features, of arms and waists. The headdresses are magnificent. The plays which they interpret are the great religious dramas that have come down through classical Indian literature. For this reason there is a wealth of characters for their plays. A hundred and twenty shadow actors is not an unusual number for the *dilang,* or master, to manage to the music of the orchestra. Branson de Cou, famous traveler and lecturer, has made a motion picture of a Javanese shadow play in which one can see not only the shadow figures, but the master manipulating them, the orchestra playing, and the audience applauding. He has also made records of the music which accompanies the play.

India is known to have brought the shadow play to a high degree of perfection, especially in religious drama. Today, however, the shadow play has almost disappeared from India except in out-of-the-way districts to the south and east, bordering on Malabar, Tamil and Cochin, where they are now given with other entertainments during festival seasons. The plays are continued from evening to evening during a week or even a month.

At the opening of each performance shadow narrators acquaint the audience with the previous incidents of the play. The story is well known to all and is chanted in unison or responsively.

Skillful manipulation of the figures is no longer considered important. The shadow screen is lighted by the flickering light of camphor burning in pieces of hollow bamboo. The few old players who travel from place to place with their worn-out shadow figures and manuscripts, scarcely realize that they have played their part in a great tradition.

One may follow the shadow play to Persia, Turkey

and Greece. Shadow plays are occasionally to be found in the Turkish coffeehouses in our country where old Karagheus, or Black Eyes, is still the rogue and hero.

Among the many treasures that came from China to England and France during the seventeenth century were shadow figures. In France the Chinese shadow plays gained royal favor, while in England they were adapted to the popular plays of the time. That clever showman, Powell, used "motions" or shadows in his "old creation of the world with the addition of Noah's flood, in 1641."

Modern European artists have not been slow to see the possibilities of this art. In Germany, Lotta Reininger, with infinite patience and skill, cut out thousands of artistic shadow figures and appropriate settings for the story of Prince Achmed in *The Arabian Nights*. From these cut-out scenery and figures a remarkable motion picture has been made and set to music. The American rights to this film were purchased by the Harvard Film Foundation, and it can be secured at a very modest rental.

Just as the Chinese shadow plays traveled to France in the seventeenth century, so today they have come to our country, and while we have no exclusive royal audience to give them favor, they are now known in a much wider circle. A great debt is due to Pauline Benton for the introduction of the Chinese shadow theater to the attention of American audiences.

Some years ago Miss Benton saw the collection of Chinese shadow figures brought together by Dr. Laufer in the Field Museum of Chicago and was inspired with the desire to see a real shadow performance. Later, on a visit to China, her wish was gratified. Here is her description of the first performance which she saw.

In a courtyard of a restaurant on a summer evening, the stage was set up and the venerable shadow players entertained the guests as they ate at small tables under a straw matting awning. The miniature theatre was draped with embroidered silk hangings and across the proscenium was stretched a sheet of pure white gauze. Against this screen, illuminated from behind by a strong lamp, the transparent colored figures were made to perform with amazing dexterity by the leading manipulator, known as "Mr. Under-the-Lamp." The figures were elaborately jointed and their graceful manipulation was accomplished by means of slender bamboo handles to be operated from below out of range of the lamp's shadow casting light. "Under-the-Lamp's" assistant stood behind him, ready on the instant to supply new characters and return them to a sort of wire clothesline where they hung in order to await their next cues. The third member of the company was the "one-man orchestra," who played a stringed instrument, a flute, drums, cymbals, and chanted the lines. He was a venerable old soul with an engaging toothless smile and silvery queue wound around his half bald pate. It was said he had seen service in some of the distinguished princely homes. At the conclusion of the performance, the guests enjoyed their visit behind the scenes and marveled to see such a delightful entertainment trundled away in a few chests.

In Peiping, I also met an aged carver, who had inherited the art from past generations and made the shadow figures used for these productions. From childhood he had seen and taken part in the plays, becoming as familiar with the text as the average American child is with Mother Goose. He had entertained with his art in the courtyards of princely homes and had even presented his plays for the late Empress Dowager. The figures were carefully made, carved in minute detail from thin layers of donkey-skin parchment and colored with transparent dyes. Each character was made especially for the part he was to play for his costume must be as authentic to the true characteristic traditions of the theater as those of human actors.

After Miss Benton's return she was engaged in work with students from different countries. A group of Chinese students borrowed shadow figures for a program they were called upon to present. She helped them with the program and became so fascinated with the interest of the audience and the opportunity for the study of Chinese culture which the shadow figures and their play offered that she devoted every spare moment to the study of the Chinese shadow theater. About this time, she made the acquaintance of Lee Ruttle, a young actor, who had performed with some of the little-theater groups in New York and was an original member of the Provincetown theater group. Together they built a stage, worked out lighting effects and perfected the manipulation of the figures. Through an aunt of Miss Benton's, a resident of Peiping, they corresponded with an old Chinese player who had been the official shadow player at the court of the late Dowager Empress. They asked him numerous questions. Last year Miss Benton returned to Peiping and spent several months studying with him, learning his tricks of skillful manipulation, collecting new manuscripts, shadow figures and musical instruments. She made a trip to the country districts where shadow plays are most prevalent, and had an opportunity of watching the best shadow performers in North China.

Music, of course, was important. William Russell, known as a composer of modern pieces and a student of Oriental music, arranged and synchronized music for Miss Benton's plays. He has brought back into use melodic folk tunes played on two-stringed violins, the moon guitar, and the clear tinkling "Yung-Chin." He has also brought into the play, in a colorful form, the conventional music of the Chinese theater, such as sonorous gongs (*lo*) which announce the entrance of a male character, and the small high-pitched gongs (*hsiao-lo*) which tell that a female character is about to enter.

The latest member of the company is King Lan Chew, a Chinese dancer who as mistress of ceremonies introduces the plays to the American audience, making any part, that might seem strange and unfamiliar, comprehensible to them. She also presents Chinese dance numbers which give the audience an opportunity to see how very natural and lifelike shadow figures are in all their movements.

The visit of the Red Gate Players to the Cleveland Museum of Art was a real inspiration to all those who were interested in the shadow theater. We came to feel that we were not innovators, but very humble workers in a great tradition. We found that we had much material on hand to carry on our work. There were the material things such as unbleached muslin, white wrapping paper and other excellent papers for screens. There was modern lighting, making it possible to light a screen of any size with safety. There were modern lanterns for throwing the light onto the screen. In our libraries we found a wealth of literary material, not only Chinese and other Oriental tales, but European and American folk tales. In fact, a world of dramatic literature just waiting to find a new form of interpretation.

Moreover, there is a vast new audience at hand devoted to the shadow world of the movie theater. Here is an art that cannot only draw upon every form of dramatic literature, but one that requires skill, ingenuity and taste, and that will give great pleasure to a wide range of ages and interests. Moreover, it can be done at a minimum of expense. Here is a kind of theater that includes music and dance as well as dramatic reading, that uses color and that will never forget for a moment the beauty of design. An old art and yet a new one has come to challenge us, and we pass it along to you.

Chinese shadow figure of a dragon

Behind the screen with the Red Gate Shadow Players

Chinese shadow figures. Cleveland Museum of Art

Chinese shadow figure, "The Elephant's Child."
Cleveland Museum of Art

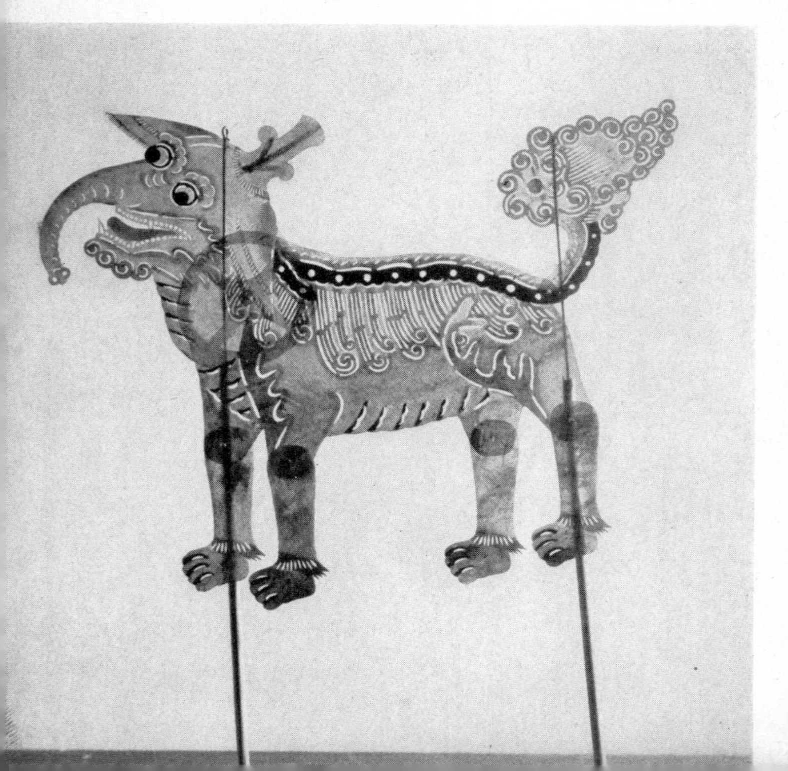

# PART I

## Cut-out Shadow Plays

# CHAPTER I

## Selecting the Shadow Play

BEFORE WE MAKE any shadow figures or the screen, we must select a play. Now choosing the shadow play is quite as important as making the figures or the screen. If you have decided to use a shadow play that has already been written, you may wish to choose one of the plays in this book. However, you may not find just the one that you are looking for and may decide that you would like to write your own play. Perhaps you are interested in Robin Hood and his merry men and their adventures—or you may wish to make a play about the pioneers who with courage and perseverance crossed the plains in their lumbering covered wagons. You may know the story which you wish to dramatize very well indeed, and feel that you can describe the characters clearly and make them talk easily and naturally. Nevertheless, there are several important questions you should ask yourself before beginning to write your play:

*First.* For whom is the play to be given? If for little children it must be a story that they can easily follow, such as a simple folk tale, a fable or fairy tale. This kind of story, when made into a play and well acted, will interest older people as well as children. Everyone loves Kipling's "The Elephant's Child," a jolly, lively shadow play given by the Red Gate Shadow Players.

*Second.* Does the story have action? For the interest of the audience is held by the movement of the figures on the screen quite as much as by what they say. Robin Hood sitting under the greenwood tree telling his men about the day's adventures would make a very dull play, but to show Robin Hood and his merry men in the midst of the day's adventure would be interesting and exciting. The play must have plenty of action to hold the attention of the audience.

*Third.* Does the story present a problem or dramatic plan? This is necessary for the reason that a problem is a struggle and everyone is interested in a struggle, wishing to see the result. For instance, the problem or struggle in "Treasure Island" is whether or not Jim can win the treasure. In the "Siege of Troy" it is whether or not the Greeks will win against the Trojans. The problem or, shall we say, struggle makes everything the actors do and say of interest to those watching. Even in as simple a play as "The Three Little Pigs" there is a very absorbing problem —as to whether the wolf will win or the little pigs.

*Fourth.* There is the question of the size of the group giving the play. Some plays require a great many characters, others just a few. If your group is small, you should not try to give a play with a great many characters, at least not for your first play. Let us say that you have six boys and girls in your group, and your story has ten characters; if several of the characters are minor ones, four members of the group could

A Chinese shadow figure and its shadow

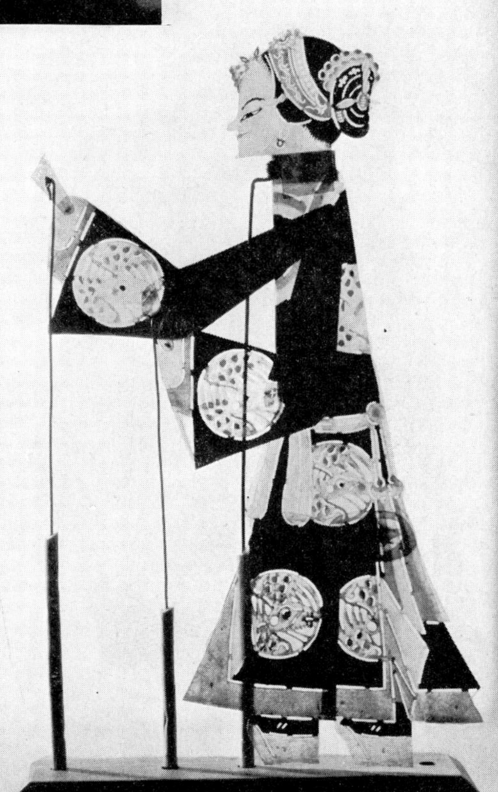

Another Chinese shadow figure

Turkish shadow figures. Cleveland Museum of Art

easily manage to play two parts each. Let us say that you have chosen for your play that humorous old folk tale "The Traveling Musicians of Bremen." How would one go about dramatizing this story? It is not difficult at all. First, make a list of the most important incidents in the story. Second, decide upon the number of scenes that you think necessary for your play. Third, decide upon the number of characters required for these scenes. Your outline will be somewhat as follows:

INCIDENT I—Donkey on the road.
INCIDENT II—Donkey meets the Dog.
INCIDENT III—Donkey and Dog meet Cat.
INCIDENT IV—Donkey, Dog and Cat meet Cock.
INCIDENT V—The animals decide to become traveling musicians and leave home.
INCIDENT VI—In the wood they see a light.
INCIDENT VII—Donkey looks through the window of Robbers' home.
INCIDENT VIII—Donkey, Dog, Cat and Cock break through the window.
INCIDENT IX—Robbers flee with fright.
INCIDENT X—Animals devour the feast and settle themselves for the night.
INCIDENT XI—One Robber returns.
INCIDENT XII—He is scratched by the Cat.
INCIDENT XIII—Bitten by the Dog.
INCIDENT XIV—Kicked by the Donkey.
INCIDENT XV—And the Cock cries, "Cock-a-doodle-doo!"
INCIDENT XVI—The Robber flees to his companions and tells them a witch clawed him, a demon stabbed him, a giant beat him with a club, and a terrible spirit on the roof screamed, "Throw him up to me!"

SCENE I—The Roadside.
SCENE II—In the Woods.
SCENE III—The Robbers' House.

CHARACTERS—Donkey, sad and thin, but undefeated.
Dog, old, tired, hungry.
Cat, old and tired.
Cock, full of excitement.

Now under the unhappy circumstances at the beginning of the play, what would you imagine the Donkey would say? Do you think he would begin something like this?

"Alas and alack, this is a sad day for me. I am old and weary. To think of all the heavy loads I have carried for my master, and now he turns me out to die. What an ungrateful wretch he is! How fortunate that I still have my wits and my beautiful musical voice! He haw, he haw! I'll go to Bremen and become the town's musician. Now who comes here, looking so forlorn and downcast?"

Do you get an impression of the old Donkey's appearance and his disposition from his words? If you do, the words are right; that is, they are "in character." You see, there must be a harmonious relationship between the appearance, the action and the word, otherwise the character will not seem natural, will not come to life. The more you know about playwriting the more you will realize that it is not enough to be familiar with just the plot of the story; the most important thing is character. If you know your characters so well that they seem to talk of themselves, you will find playwriting lots of fun.

There are many fine stories that would make good, entertaining shadow plays. Perhaps you know just where to get the story you want to use, but perhaps you would like to adventure into the field of books unfamiliar to you.

The list of books which you will find on pages 191–198 will give you many stories selected for adaptation to shadow plays. Some of these are old friends, but some are new ones worth knowing.

## CHAPTER II

# Producing Cut-out Shadow Plays

THE PLAY has been written or selected. Now we are ready to take the first step toward producing it. We must have a screen and a light. Scenery, too, will be needed, and, of course, the shadow figures.

If we organize our group so that the responsibility is divided among the various members, and each member realizes that even the smallest thing he is given to do is worth doing well, we will soon see how much can be accomplished through co-operation.

There are several different kinds of material that will make satisfactory screens. The screen may be made of a white bed sheet, unbleached muslin or a light-weight cotton stuff such as nainsook, tightly stretched and tacked to a wooden frame. It may be made of a white window shade or of white paper, oiled, dried and then shellacked.

The simplest kind of a shadow screen would be a piece of an old sheet pinned in a doorway at a convenient height for the players. The opening below the screen should be covered with heavier material to conceal the players from the audience. The scenery and properties could be cut from heavy wrapping paper and pinned to the screen.

It is always possible to give a shadow play extemporaneously, and it is surprising how much talent will appear when a group decide to give a play with just the materials that are at hand. The audience enjoys this kind of informal entertainment quite as much as the players. It is a challenge to wit and ingenuity.

If you decide to paint the scene upon the screen, a different screen will have to be used for each scene, and each screen stretched and tacked upon a frame. Here is a sketch of a standard, with grooves to hold

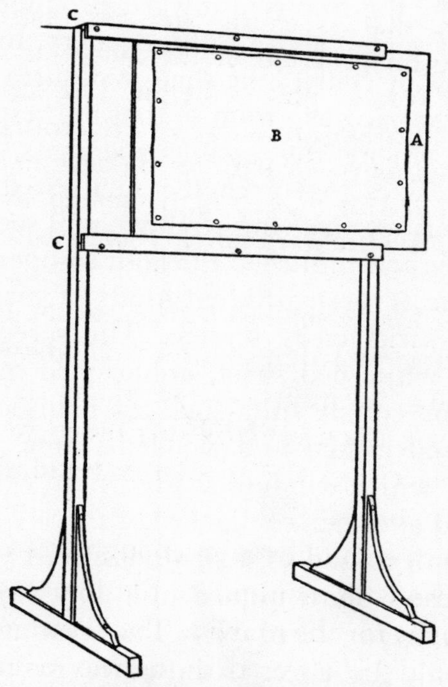


The frame *a*, upon which is fastened the translucent paper or cloth *b*, slides in and out of the standard at the grooves *c, c*.

the frames. When the scene is changed, the frame is easily removed and replaced by the next one.

There is another type of screen, which is more difficult to make and to manage. It can be of any length, depending upon the number of scenes in the play. The screen for "The Carnival of Animals" was forty-two feet long, painted in colors, and so designed that one scene merged into another when it was rolled or unrolled on vertical rollers at either side of the proscenium opening, which was three by five feet wide.

The Red Gate Shadow Players use a screen and proscenium that is exotic and fascinating, which touches the imagination of the audience and makes them eager for the play to begin. The scenery is not painted on the screen. There are separate set pieces, trees, mountains, rocks, temples, palaces and furniture. They are fixed in place on the screen by means of needle points which are quickly and easily caught in place.

Behind Chinese shadow screens, at the lower edge, there is a narrow ledge on which the player rests the feet of his shadow figure. His set pieces and properties may also rest upon it. It is this ledge which makes walking, kneeling, sitting and a hundred and one movements possible.

The screen should be high enough from the floor to permit those who manipulate the figures to stand or sit without being seen above the lower edge of the screen by the audience. If those who manage the figures are going to sit, a bench is to be preferred to chairs.

How much in the way of scenery and properties should one have for a shadow play? We shall all agree, I am sure, that the characters in the play are more important than the settings.

If the screen is crowded, there will be confusion and disorder, and the actions of the figures will be lost. There should be a sense of space, giving the figures room in which to move across the screen. It is the silhouette of the figure, its actions and the voice of the actor that transport your spectators to the land of make-believe.

If the scenes are well designed, they will add to the interest and the beauty of the play. In "Tom, the Water Baby" how much the scene adds to the play! This is also true of "The Carnival of Animals," as you can see from the pictures. The scenes were a harmonious setting for the figures and for the mood of the plays.

When the scene is painted on a paper screen, black waterproof ink and transparent water colors are used. These same materials, also dyes used as one would use water colors, are practical for thin cotton screens. Before the colors are applied, a sizing should be brushed over the material to prevent the dyes or water colors from running or merging.

You can experiment by painting your scenes in color on pieces of glass cut to the size of a lantern slide. Use transparent water colors that are made especially for coloring slides and photographs. It is sometimes necessary to mix the colors with a small amount of transparent glue. These painted glass scenes when projected through a lantern onto the screen are very effective.

What makes a scene beautiful? It is the composition, that is, the arrangement of the masses of dark and light, the contour of these masses and the distribution of color. If you understand the principles of balance, rhythm and harmony, you will enjoy designing the scenes.

One tree, characteristic of its kind, well drawn and well placed, will please and satisfy your audience more than three or five trees carelessly drawn and filling up the space. How much the Chinese artist can tell us about the beauty of the rock pine with a few carefully chosen lines!

The Chinese shadow players have learned that by the power of suggestion an audience can be made to imagine much more than they actually see. The skillful painting of a great rock in the foreground and a line or two for the far-distant horizon will suggest to the audience miles of rocky coastline and a stretch of ocean. Their scenery and properties are cut from donkey, goat or other skins; they are fairly stiff without being inflexible. They are elaborately decorated by incising with a sharp knife all details and pattern. Then they are brilliantly colored, and become translucent when light passes through them.

You can substitute paper for the skins of animals. After you have painted and decorated your properties, rub linseed oil on the back, then several hours later shellac on both sides.

Let us always keep in mind that the scenery and the properties are not an end in themselves; they are to help the figures tell the story. They create the environment.

There are a number of different ways of making the

figures. Perhaps you will invent a new one. There are two kinds of shadow figures: the opaque, made of cardboard, metal or thin wood, casting a black shadow; and the translucent, made of paper parchment, celluloid or cellophane, casting a form in color.

The size of the figure depends upon the size of the screen. When you have once decided upon a scale of measurement, be very careful to keep everything, figures, scenery and properties, to that scale. If you do not do this, you will destroy the illusion which you wish to create. When you have decided upon the height of the figure you are going to make, take pencil, crayon or paint and make a sketch, side view, actual size.

As shadow figures present but one silhouette, that of the profile, throughout the play, it naturally follows that this should be the most characteristic one. The shape of the nose, the chin and the head, the hands, the feet and the body must all portray a particular character. Each figure should be distinctive, sharply drawn, decisive in line, emphasizing individuality.

The sketch will be your pattern. Let us imagine that you are to make the donkey for "The Traveling Musicians of Bremen." What is he expected to do? Move his jaw when he talks, move his tail, his ears and his legs when he walks. How can this be done? The sketch on page 28 will help you. See, he even blinks his eye when he moves his jaw! If your figures are to be opaque, then use heavy construction paper or stiff cardboard that is not too heavy. You will need the following materials: stiff, light-weight cardboard or two-ply strathmore paper, two-pronged metal paper fasteners, pieces of wood a half inch wide by twelve to fifteen inches long (you will find half-inch screen molding split lengthwise very satisfactory), varied thicknesses of wire, and gummed paper about an inch in width, a pair of scissors, strong linen thread, a razor blade and a sharp knife.

Cut the figure apart where it is to be jointed, trace

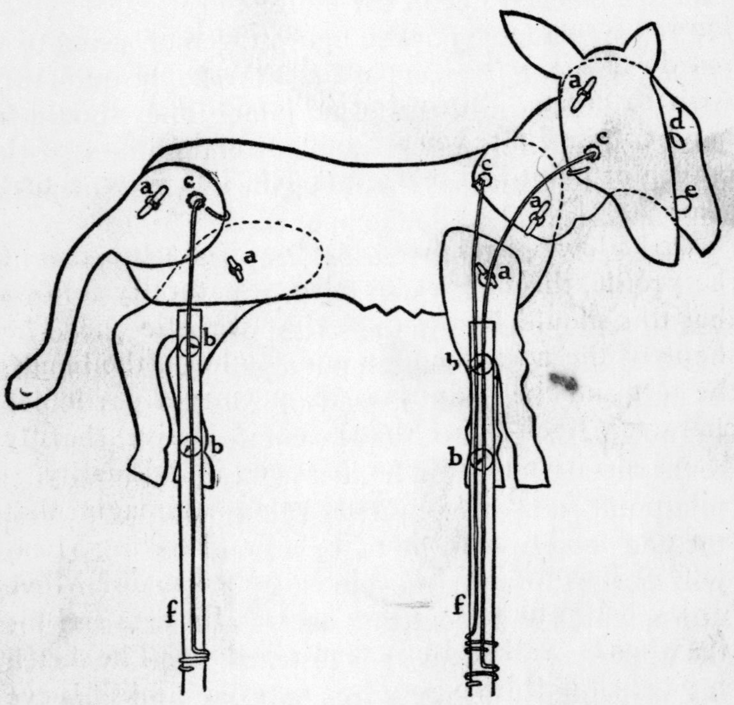


Moving parts are pivoted with paper fasteners *a*. Wires running up the sticks *f* to move the tail, neck and jaw are looped through the eyelets *c*. Thumb tacks *b* or glue may be used to fasten the figure to the sticks. Pivot points should be eyeletted before inserting the fasteners; for greater ease in working, it is sometimes well to let the head of a fastener come between two parts as at *e*. The movement of the jaw piece blinks the eye which is cut at *d*.

the parts onto the heavier paper or cardboard, allowing for one half inch overlap at joints. You will see from the sketch that the hole for the operating wire is placed either to the right or the left of the two-pronged metal paper fastener that fastens the two parts of the figure together. This allows for leverage. In place of the metal fastener you can use linen thread, knotted on each side of the figure.

When you have put the figure together, using two-pronged paper fasteners or linen thread, be quite sure that there is no stiffness at the joints. They should be loose enough for easy movement. Haughtiness, awkwardness and stiffness should be the result of intention and not an accident due to poor construction.

If metal fasteners are used, keep the prongs on the side of the figure that will be away from the screen so that it will not catch in the screen or the properties.

After the figure has been put together, glue the stick to the body. It should extend up to the waist to give support to the figure. Now fasten the operating wires to the metal eyelets and let them extend down the stick to a point four or five inches below the figure, wrap the end loosely once or twice around the stick; this will permit an easy movement of the wire, up and down, which will move that part of the body to which the upper end of the wire is fastened. If you are making birds and fish, use wires only for operating the figures. The drawing will make this clear.

Lighting your screen is an adventure in itself. You may discover new effects that will surprise and delight you. It was by accident that a group of children, working on a scene in which a ship was to be shown sailing

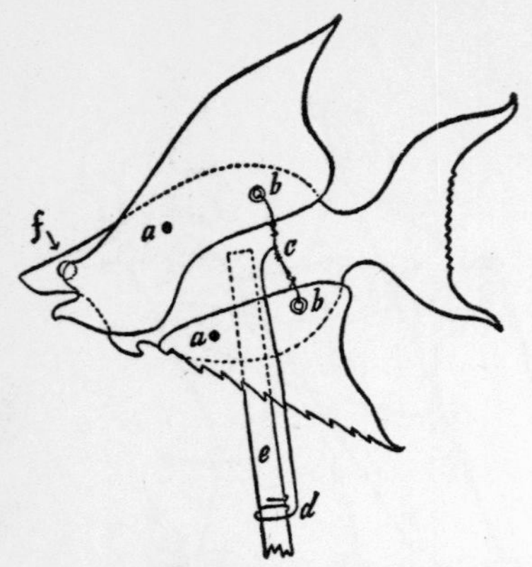


THIS shadow fish is cut from three pieces of cardboard. The pieces are assembled and pivoted at *a, a,* with paper fasteners. Eyelets *b, b,* inserted in top and bottom pieces, are connected by a thin wire. At point *c* on this wire a heavier wire is firmly fastened and run down and wound loosely about, holding stick *e* at point *d.* By moving this wire up and down, the fish's fins simulate a swimming motion, and at the same time the eye *f* opens and closes. The holding stick is firmly glued to the back of the center section.

Six pieces of cardboard form this water buffalo. With a paper fastened at *a,* the head is pivoted to the body. Likewise at *b* and *c* each pair of legs is pivoted. Holding sticks *d* and *e* are glued firmly to a front and back leg. From eyelet *f* in the head, a wire is run down and wound loosely around stick *b* at *i.* By moving this wire up and down, head movement is accomplished. From eyelets *g* and *h* in feet, wires run to sticks *e* and *d* and are firmly fastened there. By bringing sticks together and drawing them apart, a walking motion is obtained.

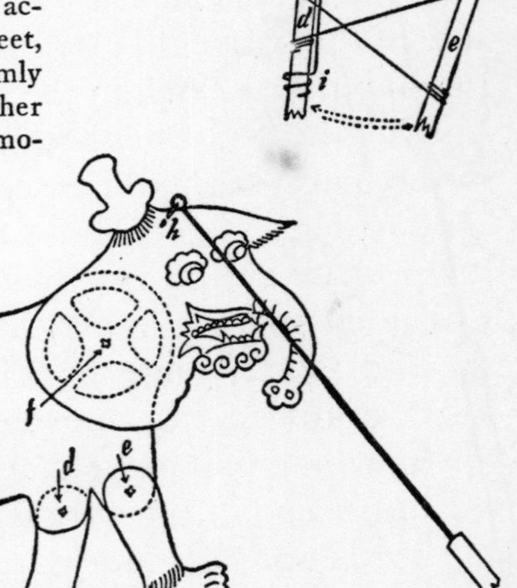


This amusing Chinese shadow elephant consists of body, head, tail and four legs. The original is made of translucent parchment, with the details executed with piercing and color. The pivots, *a, b, c, d, e* and *f* consist of stout linen thread run through and firmly knotted on each side. The holding wires are sewed with loops of thread at points *g* and *h.* Note the "wheel" construction at the neck joint, insuring smooth operation with a minimum of light-obscuring thickness.

The charming Chinese shadow woman again employs the same "wheel" joint device as the elephant. Notice that at *a* and *b* the pivots are off center toward the back. This allows for a freer fall of the parts when the figure is walked on the ledge of the shadow screen. The collar *c* is firmly attached to the body and serves as an anchorage for the holding wire which is sewed to it.

Very flexible and fierce is the Chinese shadow dragon. Two of its legs are part of the body. The other two are parts of the head and tail respectively. Here again the "wheel" is employed. The holding wires are sewed at points *a* and *b*.

upon the sea, discovered that by holding the cardboard ship stationary, about eighteen inches or more back from the screen, and then moving the light slowly from one side to the other, parallel with the screen, an illusion of the ship's sailing upon a moving sea was created.

How this accidental effect touches the imagination! Why not make a caravan cross the desert, or herds of buffalo cross the plains with Indians riding hard upon them?

The strength of the light depends upon the size of the screen, also upon the effect you wish to achieve. The stronger the light the sharper will be the shadows. If you wish to experiment with the illusion that softened shadows give, use bulbs of lesser wattage. The placing of the light behind the screen depends upon the size of the screen. For a large screen the distance will be greater than for a small screen.

The boy or girl with patience, imagination and skill will discover many things that will be of practical value.

The Chinese shadow figures are the most beautiful that have ever been made. We could never hope, in any way, to come up to their exquisite standard of perfection. However, we can make use of their method of constructing the figure, the scenery and the properties, and gain a great deal by doing so. Can you imagine how very appropriate their shadow play technique would be for plays based on the Indian lore and legends of the Southwest—where the color in rocks, earth and sky, in the costumes, pottery and weavings, is so rich and varied?

## CUT-OUT SHADOW PLAYS

If you would like to try your hand at constructing this type of figure, read the introduction over again, and you will be much better acquainted with Chinese shadow drama. Then read the following description written by the curator of Oriental art of the Detroit Institute of Art, Mr. Benjamin March:

> Shadows! No sombre featureless disembodied forms, no flat black silhouettes; but scenes that glow with the rich colouring of stained glass windows, bright-hued little people who live and move in a world of radiance diffused and softened through a paper screen. . . . The actors of the Chinese shadow drama are made of a kind of parchment of donkey skin so treated that they are stiff without being inflexible. The figures are cut out with sharp knives, and details of costume and feature are delicately incised, so that the pattern is complete and often very elaborate before any color is added. The parchment is translucent and is painted with red, green, yellow, blue and black dye in a conventionally realistic manner. The articulation of the figures is very deftly arranged. Joints occur at the shoulders, elbows, wrists, hips and knees, and bits of thread are the pivots. The wrists are especially limber, for to the finger tips are fastened the wire rods that animate the hands and arms, and the hand gestures are of great importance. The upper parts of the thigh pieces, where they overlap the body, are so cut that they have as much open work as possible, and are often uncolored, for otherwise the extra thickness at the hip would make an unpleasant and unnatural dark area. The whole body is supported at the neck by a collar of parchment to the front of which the wire control is sewn. . . . Many of the faces are merely outlined in order that the full passage of light may give them a luminous whiteness.

The pages of drawings will give you an excellent idea of the mechanics of the Chinese shadow figures. If you should choose to make this type of figure, you will be amazed to find it capable of a great deal of action and varied postures. In place of the donkey skin you can use two-ply strathmore paper or other stiff paper, the incised pattern can be cut with a sharp knife or razor blade, or a darning needle can be used for perforating the designs. Use colored inks, dyes or transparent water colors for color. Outline the profile and accent the features and any detail of the costume that you wish to make black with India ink or black lacquer. Rub linseed oil on the back of each section, allow to dry, then shellac. The black lacquer will strengthen the contour and also make the color more brilliant.

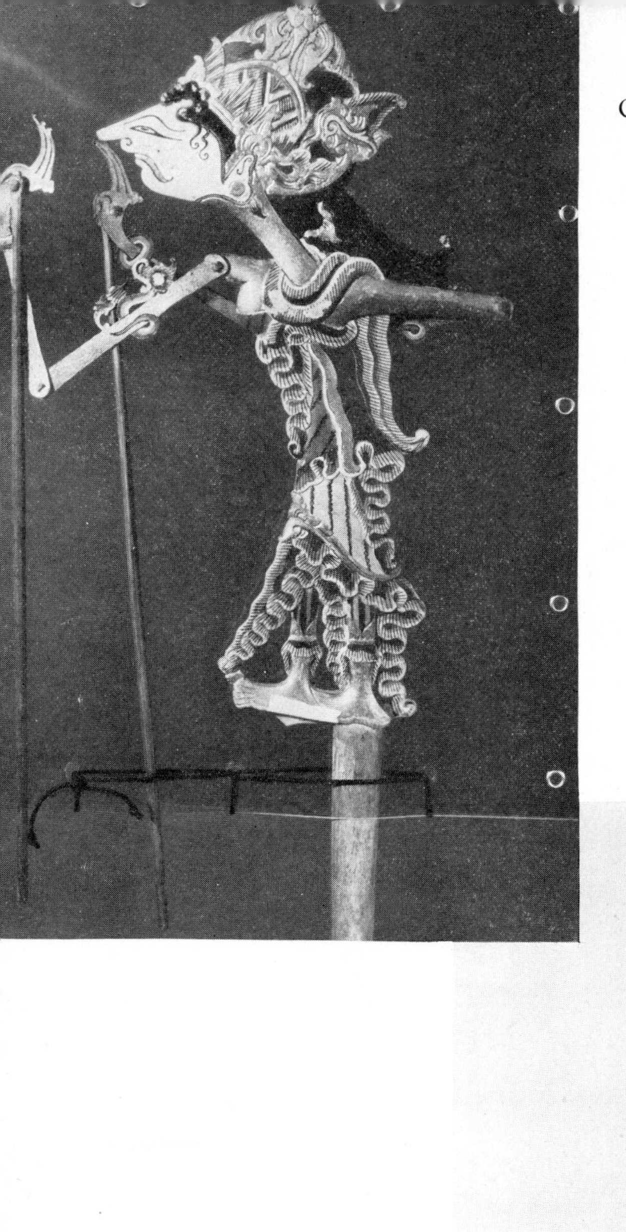

Javanese shadow figures.
Cleveland Museum of Art

A group of children giving "The Three Bears"

"The Three Bears"

A Group of Cut-out Shadow Plays Requiring Few Characters and Simple Handling:

THE THREE BEARS
THE FOX, THE MOUSE AND THE LITTLE RED HEN
THE TIGER AND THE BRAHMIN
THE LION, THE FOX AND THE BEASTS
THREE LITTLE PIGS
BLACK FACE

# THE THREE BEARS

## SCENE I

*The Three Bears' House*

GREAT BIG BEAR [*growls*] : What a hot day this is!
MIDDLE-SIZED BEAR : It may be cooler in the woods.
WEE LITTLE BEAR : Let us go to the woods, then, and find some blackberries.
GREAT BIG BEAR : A fine idea, Little Bear.
MIDDLE-SIZED BEAR : But first I must make a nice pot of porridge, so that we'll have something good to eat when we come home. I'll not be long about it.
GREAT BIG BEAR AND WEE LITTLE BEAR : Can't we help you?
MIDDLE-SIZED BEAR : Yes, Father Bear, you may stir up the fire, and, Little Bear, you may bring me a handful of salt, and then we shall be ready to go in no time.
WEE LITTLE BEAR [*singing*] :

Hey diddle diddle, the cat and the fiddle,
The cow jumped over the moon.
The little dog laughed to see such sport
And the dish ran away with the spoon.

MIDDLE-SIZED BEAR [*making gestures of cooking and stirring at the fireplace*] : Now then, this big bowl is for you, Father Bear, and this middle-sized bowl is for me, Mother Bear, and this little wee bowl is for you, Little Bear. Now let us take our walk while the porridge cools.
WEE LITTLE BEAR : Goodie, goodie, now let us go and pick some blackberries.

GREAT BIG BEAR: I'll take a book so that Mother Bear and I can read a story.

[*Father Bear, Mother Bear and Little Bear go out humming. As the humming dies away, Goldilocks is heard at a distance, singing. As Goldilocks comes near, she stops singing.*]

GOLDILOCKS [*off stage*]: Where am I? Surely this is not the way home. Oh! What a nice little house. I wonder who lives here. [*Raps on the door. No one answers.*] I should like to go in. [*Enters from right.*] Oh, what a nice, cozy place. [*Sniffs.*] I smell porridge. How hungry it makes me. I must taste it. [*Tastes Father Bear's porridge.*] Oh, this is too hot. [*Tastes Mother Bear's porridge.*] This is too cold. [*Tastes Baby Bear's porridge.*] Now this is just right [*eating*]. How good it is! Why, I have eaten it all up. [*Pause.*]

What comfortable-looking chairs! I think I'll rest in this one. [*Sits down in Father Bear's chair.*] But it is much too large. [*Goes to Mother Bear's chair.*] I think I'll try this one. [*Tries it.*] It is much too hard. Oh, what a dear little chair. [*Goes over to Baby Bear's chair and sits down. She is frightened. The child who has been holding the seat of the chair in its place now pulls it down, leaving the chair without a seat.*] What have I done? Broken it all to pieces! [*Slowly.*] I really ought to be going home. [*Pause.*] But I do wonder what is up those stairs. I think I'll go up and see.

[*Goldilocks goes upstairs at right.*]

## SCENE II

*Upstairs in the Three Bears' House*

GOLDILOCKS [*enters left*]: Oh! what a nice bedroom this is. What a great big bed. How sleepy I am. I think

I'll climb into this bed and take a nap. [*Climbs into the great big bed.*] My! how hard it is. I couldn't sleep here. [*Climbs out of the bed and goes over to the middle-sized bed.*] I think I shall try this one. [*She climbs up on the middle-sized bed.*] This is much too soft. I could never sleep here. But over there is a little wee bed that looks just right. I think I'll try that one. [*Goldilocks climbs off the middle-sized bed and gets into the wee little bed.*] Oh! This is just right. Now I can take my nap.

[*Turn off lights. Take down Scene II and again put up Scene I.*]

## SCENE III

*The Three Bears' House*

WEE LITTLE BEAR [*calling in the distance off stage*]: I'm so hungry. Let us hurry.
[*The Three Bears enter the house at right.*]
GREAT BIG BEAR [*gruffly*]: Someone has tasted my porridge.
MIDDLE-SIZED BEAR [*gruffly*]: Someone has tasted my porridge.
WEE LITTLE BEAR [*whining*]: Someone has tasted my porridge and eaten it all up.
GREAT BIG BEAR [*very gruffly, looking at his chair*]: Someone has been sitting in my chair.
MIDDLE-SIZED BEAR [*very gruffly, looking at her chair*]: Someone has been sitting in my chair.
WEE LITTLE BEAR [*whining*]: Someone has been sitting in my chair and broken it all to pieces.
GREAT BIG BEAR [*shouting*]: Broken it?
MIDDLE-SIZED BEAR [*shouting*]: Broken it?
WEE LITTLE BEAR [*sadly*]: Broken it all to pieces.
GREAT BIG BEAR [*sternly*]: Who has done all this?
MIDDLE-SIZED BEAR [*sternly*]: Who has done all this?

[*Wee Little Bear weeps.*]

GREAT BIG BEAR: Let us go upstairs.

MIDDLE-SIZED BEAR: Let us go upstairs.

WEE LITTLE BEAR: Yes, let us go upstairs.

## SCENE IV

*Upstairs in the Three Bears' House*

[*Goldilocks is asleep in Little Bear's bed. Enter Father Bear, Mother Bear and Little Bear at left.*]

GREAT BIG BEAR [*surprised*]: Someone has been sleeping in my bed.

MIDDLE-SIZED BEAR [*surprised*]: Someone has been sleeping in my bed.

WEE LITTLE BEAR: Oh, here she is—fast asleep!

GREAT BIG BEAR: Where?

MIDDLE-SIZED BEAR: Where?

WEE LITTLE BEAR: Here in my bed.

GREAT BIG BEAR: Here?

MIDDLE-SIZED BEAR: Here?

WEE LITTLE BEAR: Yes, here she is fast asleep.

GOLDILOCKS [*sitting up*]: Oh dear! [*Frightened.*] Where am I? Where am I? [*Jumps out of the bed and out of the window.*]

[*The Three Bears go to the window and look out.*]

WEE LITTLE BEAR [*calling*]: Don't be afraid; don't run away. [*Whining.*] Come back, come back, little girl, please come back and play with me.

## THE FOX, THE MOUSE AND THE LITTLE RED HEN

CHARACTERS: Cock
Mouse
Little Red Hen
Father Fox
Mother Fox
Little Foxes

SCENE I. In the den of the Fox.
SCENE II. Home of the Little Red Hen.
SCENE III. Under tree by a stream.

### SCENE I

[*Mother Fox stirring porridge on right of screen.*]

LITTLE FOXES [*enter left, whining*]: What are we going to have for dinner today? What are we going to have for dinner today? What are we going to have for dinner today? We are so hungry.

MOTHER FOX: I am making some nice porridge for you, my children.

LITTLE FOXES: We don't like porridge, we don't like porridge. We never have anything but porridge. We want meat, we want meat. [*Enter Father Fox.*] Oh, Father Fox, we are so hungry. We want meat. We have had nothing to eat for three long days. We want meat, we want meat!

FATHER FOX: Hush, hush, my children. Let me think a moment. Ah, I have an idea. Over on yonder hill there is a little house where a cock, a mouse and a little red hen are living.

LITTLE FOX [*greedily*]: Are they nice and fat?

FATHER FOX: Yes indeed, they are nice and fat. Where is my gunny sack? I'll soon bring them home, my children.

LITTLE FOX [*bringing sack to father*]: Here it is, Father, just outside the door. Hurry back, Father, we are so hungry. We will help Mother build a fire and have everything ready when you come.

MOTHER FOX: Then bring me some nice dry wood.

[*Children may make a song for the Little Foxes to sing here.*]

## SCENE II

*Little Red Hen's house.*

LITTLE RED HEN [*sweeping*]: Who will bring in some wood?

COCK: I shall not.

MOUSE: And I shall not.

LITTLE RED HEN: Then I shall do it myself. Now who will fill the kettle?

COCK: I shall not.

MOUSE: And I shall not.

LITTLE RED HEN: Then I shall do it myself. Who will cook the breakfast?

COCK: I shall not.

MOUSE: And I shall not.

LITTLE RED HEN: Then I shall do it myself. [*Sings a song and puts breakfast on the table.*] Now who will eat the breakfast?

COCK: I will.

MOUSE: And I will.

LITTLE RED HEN: Then I will too. Now who will wash the dishes?

COCK: I shall not.

MOUSE: And I shall not.

LITTLE RED HEN: Then I will, and who will help me make the beds?

COCK: I am too tired and sleepy.

MOUSE: And so am I.

FATHER FOX: Tap, tap, tap.

MOUSE: I wonder who that can be.

COCK: Why don't you go and see?

MOUSE: Maybe it is the postman with a letter for me. [*Opens the door.*] Oh dear! Oh dear! [*Frightened. Jumps to top of chair. Fox grabs Mouse and puts him in the bag.*]

COCK [*frightened*]: Cock-a-doodle-do! [*Fox grabs Cock and puts him in the bag.*]

LITTLE RED HEN: Oh dear, what can the matter be?

FATHER FOX: You will soon find out, my fine lady. Ha-ha. [*Puts the Little Red Hen in his bag.*] What a fine supper you will all make for my little foxes.

## SCENE III

FATHER FOX [*wearily*]: Oh dear me, this sack is getting so heavy I think I must rest. Right here against this tree is a very good place. [*Drops sack and leans against tree and falls asleep.*]

MOUSE: Oh dear, if I ever get out of this sack, what a good mouse I shall be.

COCK: Oh dear, and what a good cock I shall be.

LITTLE RED HEN: Cheer up, cheer up, it is never too late to mend. Here is my little work bag. Watch what I am going to do. [*Snip, snip, she cuts a small hole in the bag.*] Now run as fast as you can and bring back a stone as large as yourself. [*Runs to the brook.*] Now I'll get a stone as large as myself and put it in the bag. Here, Little Mouse, let me help you put your stone in.

LITTLE MOUSE: Thank you, good Little Red Hen.

LITTLE RED HEN: Hurry up, Cock, and roll your stone in. Now I'll sew up the hole as quickly as I can, and we'll run home as fast as we can.

MOUSE: Oh, we'll never be cross or grumble again.

COCK: We'll light the fire and fill the kettle, we'll get the breakfast and make the beds, and you shall have a holiday and rest in the big armchair by the window. Let us hurry, let us hurry home.

OLD FOX: Well, well, I must have fallen asleep. How hungry those Little Foxes must be. I must hurry home. [*Stands up and puts sack on his shoulders and walks to the brook.*] I'll take the short way across the stream. [*In midstream he drops the sack into the water and as it sinks says sadly*]: Oh dear, there goes our dinner. Down to the bottom it goes, and nothing to take home for supper.

Two scenes from "The Fox, the Mouse and the Little Red Hen"
—a cut-out shadow play given by first-grade children

Scenes from "The Lion, the Fox and the Beasts"—a cut-out shadow play given by third-grade children

## THE TIGER AND THE BRAHMIN

CHARACTERS: A Tiger
A Stag
A Bunny
A Brahmin
A Banyan Tree
A Jackal
A Bullock

[*Scene shows a banyan tree at left, shrubs, a tree and a cage of bars at right. The tiger is in the cage.*]

TIGER [*growling*]: How hungry I am. G-r-r-r. Why did I ever come into this cage? G-r-r-r. Someone tricked me—me, the king of the jungle. If I could get out—but these bars are too strong for me to break. This floor is too strong for me to tear. It is true. I shall starve to death. G-r-r-r. [*Sweetly, as Stag enters*]: Good morning, my noble friend. I have caught myself in this stupid cage. Will you kindly lift the bar for me?

STAG: How long have you been there?

TIGER [*impatiently*]: For the past three days, and I am very hungry.

STAG: You certainly must be. And I would make you a very good breakfast, my hungry friend. Friend, did I say? But you are no friend of mine, for you have hunted my family down. I am glad to see you behind bars—stay there.
[*Goes out.*]

TIGER: *G-r-r-r.* How hollow I feel—so empty and uncomfortable. Help! Help!

BUNNY [*coming in timidly*]: Oh dear, what a dreadful sound. I'm afraid! I cannot believe my eyes! Mr. Tiger in a cage, and how hungry he looks!

TIGER [*softly*]: Welcome, my gentle Bunny. How thoughtful of you to call this morning. Somehow I got into this horrid cage, and the bar slipped down. Will you kindly raise it?

BUNNY: Oh, Mr. Tiger, I am afraid you will eat me if I let you out. You may remember you have eaten all my poor brothers and sisters. So just keep on wailing for your breakfast. Good day, Mr. Tiger.

TIGER [*roars*]: Miserable Bunny, if I ever get out, I'll eat you up in one mouthful. Oh my, that last roar was too much for me. I am growing weak—weaker every minute. What shall I do? I am still a tiger, I suppose —but I don't feel like one. G-r-r-r [*softly*].

BRAHMIN [*entering*]: What's this? Mr. Tiger in a cage!

TIGER: Oh, do I still look like a tiger? I assure you I don't feel like one.

BRAHMIN: All you need is a good breakfast.

TIGER: I am hungry, Mr. Brahmin, and if you will raise the bar to this cage, I will go away into the jungle and look for something to eat.

BRAHMIN: Are you sure you would not begin with me?

TIGER: No, no, never.

BRAHMIN: You have a very bad reputation.

TIGER: I have reformed. I shall never touch a man again. Just help me this once, good kind Brahmin, and I will show you how grateful I can be.

BRAHMIN: If I were sure you would keep your promise . . .

TIGER: I shall—I promise you. Never will I attack a man again. Just let me out.

BRAHMIN [*lifts bar of cage*]: Now then, come out, poor creature, and go your way.

TIGER: Oh, how cramped I am. Oh, how hungry I feel. I must have food. I am a tiger. G-r-r-r. I shall begin with you, Mr. Brahmin.

BRAHMIN [*in terror*]: What words are these? Your promise, your promise, Mr. Tiger.

TIGER: My promise! I did not know how hungry I was. Come, come, sir.

BRAHMIN: Stop! Not even the meanest beast would break his word. I saved your life. You must not eat me!

TIGER: But I am so terribly hungry.

BRAHMIN: Hold a minute. Let us ask four creatures to judge between us.

TIGER: But man has no friends.

BRAHMIN: But if one should be a friend to man . . .

TIGER: Then you would be safe. Come on then, begin. I am starving.

BRAHMIN [*to the Banyan Tree*]: Oh, Banyan Tree, you have heard all of our argument, now judge between us.

BANYAN TREE: Man is no friend of mine. I give him rest and refreshment beneath my boughs. I supply him with fruits from my branches, yet when I grow old he cuts me down and uses me for firewood. Man is no friend of mine.

BRAHMIN: The words of the Banyan Tree are true.

TIGER: Of course they are true. There comes a bullock.

BRAHMIN: Oh, Bullock. I saved the Tiger's life, and now he would eat me.

BULLOCK: When I was young I worked for my master faithfully and hard. Now that I am old he will kill me and use me for food. Man is certainly no friend of the Bullock.

BRAHMIN: Alas, it is true.

TIGER: Man has no friend. I am hungry. [*Growls.*]

BRAHMIN: Wait—wait. Here comes a stag.

TIGER [*in a loud voice to the Stag*]: Would you save the life of a man?

STAG: Never. My life is lived in constant fear of man. He pursues me at all seasons of the year. Man is a destroyer. Let him die.

BRAHMIN [*sadly*]: Alas, alas.

TIGER: I'll—g-r-r-r. [*Deep roar.*]

BRAHMIN [*sadly*]: I fear you are right. Alas, man has no friend.

JACKAL [*enters gaily*]: Good morning, Mr. Tiger. You look ill.

TIGER: I'm hungry. I am about to eat the Brahmin, but now that you are here——

BRAHMIN [*interrupting*]: Yes, yes, now that you are here, listen to my tale of distress. I saved the Tiger's life, and now after promising not to harm me, he is about to eat me.

JACKAL [*surprised*]: Saved the Tiger! How could a mere man do that? The Tiger is the king of the jungle!

TIGER: Of course, of course—but you see, that cage——

BRAHMIN: The Tiger was in the cage, and I let him out——

TIGER: The Brahmin lifted the bar, a very simple thing to do. He was walking along and——

JACKAL: Just a minute. My brain doesn't seem very clear this morning, and I get so confused. You say the Brahmin was in the cage, and you, Mr. Tiger, were walking——

TIGER: No, no, I was in the cage.

JACKAL: Oh yes, how stupid of me. Why didn't you walk out?

TIGER: How could I? The bar was down.

JACKAL: Pray, excuse my stupidity, but why didn't you step over it?

TIGER: Step over what?

JACKAL: The bar.

TIGER: The bar, Jackal of little brains, the bar locks the door of the cage.

JACKAL [*meekly*]: Forgive me for being so foolish. I see it all—at least I am beginning to see. If I could have been here at the time . . .

TIGER: You are wasting time. I'm hungry. [*Growls.*]

JACKAL: Patience, patience, King Tiger. If you will just

show me how it was—you say the Brahmin was in the cage——

TIGER [*shouting*] : No, no, I was.

JACKAL : Oh yes, oh yes, of course. At the back or in the front, and where was the Brahmin?

BRAHMIN : I was here.

TIGER [*leaping into cage*] : And I was here.

JACKAL : And the door——

TIGER : Was shut.

JACKAL : And the bar down.

TIGER : Now that you have everything exactly as it was—what is your answer?

JACKAL : I was just about to suggest to the Brahmin that he leave you as he found you.

BRAHMIN : Wise Jackal, I thank you.

TIGER [*roars*] : If ever I get out of this cage again, I shall eat you all. [*Growls.*]

## THE LION, THE FOX AND THE BEASTS

CHARACTERS: Old Lion
A Sheep
A Goat
A Calf
A Rabbit
A Fox

### SCENE

*Under the trees at the entrance to the Lion's cave.*

OLD LION [*groaning and stretching*]: Oh, how hungry I am. [*Groans.*] Oh, how hungry I am. I haven't had a bit to eat since I came to this old cave. [*Growls.*] These young animals here are all too quick for me. They run and hide whenever they see me coming. [*Sits up and moans.*] I'll starve to death if I can't think of a way to catch them. [*Pause.*] I have it, I have it now. I'll pretend to be sick, very sick indeed. I'll go into my cave and groan until they think I am dying. Now watch me fool them.

[*Old Lion lies down and begins moaning and groaning as though he were about to die. Enter on right a sheep and a goat.*]

SHEEP [*grazing*]: What nice, sweet, juicy grass!

GOAT [*lifting head and chewing*]: Yes, but I know a place where it is much better.

SHEEP: Where?

[*Old Lion groans and moans.*]

GOAT: Hark, what is that? Someone must be in terrible pain. Let us go and see what the trouble is.

SHEEP: Baa, baa. I'm afraid, I'm afraid. Baa, baa.

GOAT [*going to entrance of cave, surprised, says to the Sheep*]: Well, well, I can scarcely believe my eyes. It is our old King, the Lion. [*Coming near the cave.*] What is the matter with you?

[*The Lion suddenly springs upon the Goat and drags it into his cave.*]

LION: Ha, ha, ha. It pays to use your wits. I'll try this trick again.

SHEEP [*coming back again and calling*]: Where are you, Friend Goat? [*Goes near the entrance to the cave.*]

LION [*moaning softly*]: Help! Help! Help!

SHEEP: Can it be? It is our old King, the Lion. How sick he looks. I wonder if there is anything that I can do for him.

[*Lion springs on the Sheep and drags it into the cave.*]

LION: Ha, ha, ha. It surely pays to use your wits. Listen. I hear someone coming. [*Lion lies down and appears to be dead.*]

CALF [*coming along toward the cave*]: I thought I heard someone groan. Can it be the old Lion, our King? Here he lies. I do believe that he is dead.

[*Goes nearer. Lion jumps up and pounces on the Calf, drags it back into his cave.*]

LION: Ha, ha, ha. I certainly am clever. It certainly pays to use your wits. [*Lies down.*]

RABBIT [*hopping along near cave*]: Goodness! What can that be? I am so scared. But I'll try to be brave. [*Surprised.*] Oh! It is our old King, the Lion, and he is dying. [*Rabbit hops very near.*]

LION [*pouncing on the Rabbit*]: Ha, ha, ha. How stupid they all are! And how easy it is to outwit them. [*Returns to cave, lies down and groans.*]

FOX [*coming up from right, hears the groaning and stops suddenly*]: What can that be? The sound seems to come from that cave. [*Looks down.*] What a lot of footprints there are, and all leading into the cave. I must be careful here.

LION [*groaning*]: I am so sick. Please come in and help me.

FOX: Well, well, well. It is the Lion, our King. He does moan as though he were sick, but I must be very careful.

LION [*moaning louder*]: Oh, oh, oh, help, help.

FOX: Oh no, old Mr. Lion, you don't need any help. Why do all these footprints lead into your cave and none of them lead out, pray tell? I had better be on my way. Good day, sir. I find it always pays to use one's wits.

LION [*growls*]: The Fox has always been too smart for me, but—I'll get him yet. I'll get him yet.

## THREE LITTLE PIGS

CHARACTERS: Mother Pig
First Little Pig
Second Little Pig
Third Little Pig
Big Gray Wolf
Man with Straw
Man with Wood
Man with Bricks

### SCENE I

[*The screen shows at left the front door and porch of Mrs. Pig's house—a fenced-in yard, flowers, and a road going off right. Distant fields and low hills. Mother Pig and three Little Pigs before door of the house.*]

MOTHER PIG [*sadly*]: My dear little piggies, I want to talk to you.

FIRST LITTLE PIG: Are you going to tell us a story, Mother?

MOTHER PIG: No, my children, but have you noticed lately that our house seems to be growing smaller every day?

FIRST LITTLE PIG: That is because we are growing so big. I am the biggest.

SECOND LITTLE PIG: I am the biggest.

THIRD LITTLE PIG: I am the biggest of all. [*All continue to shout.*]

MOTHER PIG: Hush, my children. And have you noticed how little food there is in the cupboard?

FIRST LITTLE PIG: That is because I eat so much.

SECOND LITTLE PIG: That is because I eat so much.

THIRD LITTLE PIG: That is because I eat so much. I eat most of all. [*All shouting.*]

MOTHER PIG: Hush, my children What are we to do?

FIRST LITTLE PIG: I am big enough to build a house of my own.

SECOND LITTLE PIG: I am big enough to build a house of my own.

THIRD LITTLE PIG: I am big enough to build a house of my own, and get my own food too.

MOTHER PIG: What brave little piggies you all are!

FIRST LITTLE PIG: Oh, what fun it will be to build a house!

SECOND LITTLE PIG: Oh, what fun it will be to build a house!

THIRD LITTLE PIG: Oh, what fun it will be to build a house of my very own!

FIRST LITTLE PIG: How jolly. Let us go and find the places.

MOTHER PIG [*anxiously*]: But wait, my children. You must be careful where you go. The old Gray Wolf may be watching for you. And wherever you go, remember your good manners.

FIRST LITTLE PIG: Don't worry, Mother, we'll be careful.

SECOND LITTLE PIG: We'll be polite.

THIRD LITTLE PIG: Don't worry, Mother, we'll come back and bring you some nice yellow turnips and some juicy red apples.

MOTHER PIG [*weeps*]: You certainly are brave Little Pigs.

FIRST LITTLE PIG [*walking gaily*]: I'll take the road to the right.

SECOND LITTLE PIG: I'll take the road to the left.

THIRD LITTLE PIG: I'll go straight ahead.

[*All the Little Pigs call*]: Good-by, Mother.

MOTHER PIG: Good-by, children,

## SCENE II

[*Screen shows a nice little house made of straw near the center. A road crosses the screen from left to right. The straw house is a property made of cardboard which can be pulled down when the Wolf "blows the house down."*]

FIRST LITTLE PIG [*meeting man carrying straw*]: Please, kind sir, may I have some of your straw? I want to finish my little house.

MAN CARRYING STRAW: What a very polite little pig you are. Certainly you may have some of my straw. Help yourself.

FIRST LITTLE PIG: Oh, thank you, thank you very much. [*Begins to sing as he works on his house*]: I have almost finished my house,
I have almost finished my house,
I have almost finished my house,
Early in the morning.
[*Admiring his house*]: My house is finished at last. I think I shall go in and close my door and take a nap.

BIG GRAY WOLF [*creeping up to door and rapping*]: Hello, Little Pig. How are you today? Will you let me come in?

FIRST LITTLE PIG [*frightened voice from within house*]: No, no, by the hair of my chin, chin, chin, I won't let you come in.

BIG GRAY WOLF [*angrily*]: Little Pig, if you don't let me in, I'll huff and I'll puff and I'll blow your house in.

FIRST LITTLE PIG: No, no, I won't let you blow my house in.

BIG GRAY WOLF: We'll see about that.
[*He huffs and puffs and blows the straw house until it shakes, while the First Little Pig runs out his back door and away.*] Ha-ha! Huff! Puff! Down comes

your house. [*As the straw house tumbles down, the Wolf, growling furiously, searches for the Little Pig.*] You think you can fool me, do you? Just wait, I'll get you yet, and that fat little brother of yours too.

## SCENE III

[*Screen shows a little house made of pieces of wood and branches. A tree grows near by, a road runs across the screen from right to left. The Second Little Pig is standing beside his house. The house of wood is a property made of cardboard, which can be pulled down when the Wolf "blows the house down."*]

SECOND LITTLE PIG: Ah, what luck, here comes a man with a load of wood.
[*Enter man pulling a cart of wood.*]
Please, kind sir, may I have some of your wood? I want to finish my house.

THE WOOD MAN: What a very polite little pig you are. Certainly you may have some wood. Help yourself.

SECOND LITTLE PIG: Thank you. This is all I need to finish my door.
[*Exit Wood Man. Little Pig enters his house and begins to sing.*]
What a nice little house I have, what a nice little house I have.

BIG GRAY WOLF [*creeping up to front door and rapping*]: Hello, Little Pig, how are you today? I have brought you some nice fresh turnips. Will you let me come in?

SECOND LITTLE PIG [*trembling*]: No, no, by the hair of my chin, chin, chin, I won't let you come in.

BIG GRAY WOLF [*angrily*]: Little Pig, if you don't let me come in, I'll huff and I'll puff and I'll blow your house in.

SECOND LITTLE PIG: Please, please, don't blow down my house.

BIG GRAY WOLF: We'll see about that. Huff-f-f! Puff-f-f! [*The house shakes and falls down. The little pig escapes by the back door. The Gray Wolf rages.*] So you, too, think you can fool me. Just wait, I'll catch you and your smart little brothers yet.

## SCENE IV

[*Screen shows a nice little house of bricks, a tree or two and a road.*]

THIRD LITTLE PIG: If I just had a few more bricks, I could finish my nice little house. Oh, here comes a man with a load of bricks. Perhaps he will be kind enough to give me a few.
[*Enter a man with horse and cartload of bricks.*]
Please, kind sir, may I have a few of your bricks? I want to finish my house this morning.

MAN WITH BRICKS: What a polite little pig you are. Certainly you may have a few bricks. Help yourself.

THIRD LITTLE PIG: Thank you! Thank you!

MAN WITH BRICKS: Welcome you are. Get along, Dobbin!

THIRD LITTLE PIG [*singing*]: This will finish my house of bricks, my house of bricks,
This will finish my house of bricks, so early in the morning.
[*He goes into the house with his bricks and begins to finish his fireplace. First Little Pig, breathless, runs to the door and knocks.*]

FIRST LITTLE PIG: Brother, brother, let me in. Let me in quick.
[*Third Little Pig opens the door and takes First Little Pig in.*]

THIRD LITTLE PIG: What is the matter?

FIRST LITTLE PIG: The Big Gray Wolf blew down my house, and almost ate me.

[*Second Little Pig runs to the door and knocks.*]

SECOND LITTLE PIG: Brother, brother, let me in. Let me in quick! The Big Gray Wolf is after me.

[*Third Little Pig opens the door. Second Little Pig enters breathless and shaking.*]

Oh, the Big Gray Wolf blew down my house and threatens to catch us all.

THIRD LITTLE PIG: Don't be afraid, little brothers. Stop shaking. This house is made of bricks. Let the big bad Wolf huff and puff all day long—he can't blow this house down. Now I'll just lock the door.

[*A rap at the door. The Little Pigs stand close together.*]

BIG GRAY WOLF: Hello, Little Pig. What a fine house you have here. I thought you might like some apples this morning. May I come in?

THIRD LITTLE PIG: No! No! By the hair of my chin, chin, chin, you cannot come in.

BIG GRAY WOLF: What's that you say? You silly little pig. I'll huff and I'll puff and I'll blow your house down and I'll eat you all for my dinner.

THIRD LITTLE PIG: You can huff, and you can puff, but you can't blow my house down.

[*The Big Gray Wolf huffs and puffs, and puffs and huffs, but the little brick house does not even shake. The three Little Pigs dance about singing, "Who's Afraid of the Big Bad Wolf?" The Wolf rages at the door.*]

BIG GRAY WOLF: You think you are so smart. I'll come down your chimney and eat you yet.

[*The Wolf climbs up the roof to the chimney as the Little Pigs take the lid off the boiling kettle in the fireplace. The Wolf tumbles down the chimney into the pot. The Little Pigs begin to sing again, "Who's Afraid of the Big Bad Wolf?"*]

## BLACK FACE

*A Modern Fantasy*

Dramatized from a story by Thelma H. Bell

CHARACTERS: Black Face
Five Sheep
Shepherdess
Engineer
Station Master
Patricia
Patricia's Mother
Dog
Kitten
Shepherd
Organ-Grinder, Monkey
Little Girl
Spot
First Boy
Tom

### SCENE I

*In the meadow. Morning.*

SCENE: Scattered bushes. Log to the left. Fence stretched across foreground.

[*Shepherdess enters left, singing, followed by her sheep, who scatter about grazing. Shepherdess wears full skirts and large-brimmed hat. She carries a crook and a basket. Black Face slips behind a bush to hide. Shepherdess turns when she reaches the log. Pointing her crook at the sheep, she counts them.*]

SHEPHERDESS: One sheep, two sheep, three and four and five. There should be six sheep. Who is missing?

ONE SHEEP [*bleating*]: Bl-black Face.

SHEPHERDESS: Black Face, Black Face, where are you?

[*Black Face prances out from behind bush.*]

Black Face, you are naughty. You must not hide from me.

BLACK FACE [*bleating*]: W-why?

SHEPHERDESS: Never mind why.

[*Shepherdess dusts off the log, sits down and takes out her knitting. The sheep leap about and graze. Black Face walks along the fence. Three times he tries to put his head under the fence. He comes to the log and stands before the Shepherdess.*]

BLACK FACE [*bleating*]: Where does the little train go, the little green train that passes our meadow?

SHEPHERDESS: To the big town, my little lamb. Why do you ask such a question?

BLACK FACE: I like the little train. I should like to go with it.

SHEPHERDESS: Indeed, you cannot go. The big town is dangerous. You would get lost.

BLACK FACE: The little train would whistle to me, and I should find it again.

SHEPHERDESS: You must stay inside the fence as the other sheep do. They do not talk of traveling.

BLACK FACE: But I want to go.

SHEPHERDESS: Run along, I say. Traveling is not good for little lambs.

[*Black Face prances off. He disappears abruptly.*]

SHEEP [*bleating*]: Oh, Shepherdess, Oh, Shepherdess, Black Face has fallen into the ditch.

SHEPHERDESS [*getting up*]: The foolish lamb. I will help him. [*Shepherdess pulls up Black Face with her crook.*] You are all covered with burrs. Black Face, what will you do next?

[*Shepherdess sits down again, has lost stitch, counts stitches. Black Face goes to fence and puts his fore-feet on the rail.*]

BLACK FACE [*talking to himself*] : I walked all along the fence. There is no way to get under. But now I know that the ditch runs under the fence. When the little train comes, I can jump into the ditch. I can squeeze under the fence and climb onto the track and talk to the little train.

[*A far-off whistle sounds faintly. Black Face takes his hoofs from the rail.*] The train is coming!

SHEPHERDESS: The noonday train is coming. It is time for my lunch.

[*Shepherdess puts down her knitting. Across the back of the scene a very small train passes. The whistle grows louder. A middle-sized train crosses the scene. The Shepherdess is busy getting her lunch from the basket. She does not see Black Face slip into the ditch. Now the whistle is shrill. The full-sized train starts to cross the scene. Black Face scrambles up onto the track. The train stops.*]

BLACK FACE: Hello, little train.

[*The Engineer leans out of his cab.*]

ENGINEER: Shoo, shoo, get away, little lamb, you will be hurt.

[*Black Face climbs onto the cowcatcher, where the Engineer cannot see him.*]

ENGINEER: Did he jump down? Yes, he has gone away.

[*The Engineer clangs the bell. The train chug-chugs and moves slowly off. The Shepherdess is heard calling.*]

SHEPHERDESS: Black Face! Black Face! Stop the train! He is going away with the train. [*As the train leaves the scene, the Shepherdess can be seen waving her crook.*] Oh! Oh! Oh!

## SCENE II

*The railway station. Afternoon.*

SCENE: Station building. A small boy, whistling, passes with a dog. An organ-grinder with a monkey comes in. Patricia with her mother follows them. The monkey performs. Patricia claps her hands.

PATRICIA: Oh, Mother, he is so quaint. I should like a new pet.

MOTHER: Not a monkey, my dear. We should not know how to care for him. Come now, we must be going home.

[*The train whistle is heard.*]

PATRICIA: The train! The train is coming. Please let us stay to watch it.

MOTHER: If you stand still beside me.

[*The chug-chugging gets louder and louder.*]

PATRICIA: We shall see the engine and the Engineer first.

[*The full-sized train appears. It stops when just the engine and the cab can be seen. Black Face, with his ears blown wide, is on the cowcatcher.*]

EVERYONE: Look! Look!

PATRICIA: Mother, a lamb on the train! A black-faced lamb!

[*Black Face jumps down. He walks gaily to Patricia and lifts his head to her hand. She pats him. Black Face bleats.*]

He likes me. Please may I take him home for my pet?

MOTHER: My dear child, he must belong to someone.

PATRICIA: But he was all alone.

MOTHER: I'll ask the Engineer. [*Approaches Engineer, who stands beside engine.*] Pardon me, do you know to whom this lamb belongs?

[*The Engineer scratches head, thinks, shakes head.*]

ENGINEER: No ma'am, I don't know where he came from.

Looks like he dropped from the sky. This is a passenger train. We don't pull cattle cars.
[*The Station Master comes up.*]

STATION MASTER: Pardon me, ma'am, is he yours?

MOTHER: No, he came in on the cowcatcher of the train.

PATRICIA: He doesn't seem to belong to anyone. I should like so much to have him.

STATION MASTER: He certainly likes you, little miss. You had better keep him.

PATRICIA: Oh, thank you. Come, little Black Face, you are mine now. I'll take you home to play with my dog and my kitty.
[*Black Face trots beside her as they move off.*]

## SCENE III

*The front yard of Patricia's home. House in rear. Fence with gate across the front. Morning.*
[*Patricia enters right, followed by Black Face.*]

PATRICIA: Did you have a pleasant sleep in the barn, my Black Face?
[*Black Face bleats.*]
Now we can play. Here come my dog, Tippy, and my kitten. The kitten's name is Fluff. Here, Fluff. Here, Tippy.
[*Dog and kitten romp in.*]
Here is your new playmate, Black Face. Come and welcome him.
[*The kitten stops short. Her tail goes up. She spits. The dog barks. The kitten springs upon Black Face's back.*]
Oh, Kitty, don't scratch Black Face. Be careful. You will fall. Hold fast to his curls.
[*Black Face runs around, jumps up and down. Patricia rescues Fluff.*]
Silly Fluff, Black Face is a friend.

[*Mother enters right, calls.*]

MOTHER: We are going for a drive, Patricia. Your lamb will be safe inside the fence.

[*Black Face raises an ear and looks mischievous.*]

PATRICIA: Good-by. Don't quarrel. Eat the fresh grass, Black Face. I shall play with you before luncheon.

[*Patricia goes out right. Fluff spits at Black Face and scampers off left. The dog barks at Black Face and runs out. Black Face looks around. He is alone. He nibbles the grass. He paws the ground restlessly with his hoof. He is lonely. He goes to the fence and puts his forefeet on the rail.*]

BLACK FACE: I wonder what the sheep in the meadow are doing. The little Shepherdess is knitting, I am sure.

[*A sound of bleating is heard. Black Face looks up the road. Some sheep appear.*]

Baa-aa! Where are you going?

FIRST SHEEP: Baa-aa, I don't know. Early this morning the Shepherd brought us from our field on to the road.

SECOND SHEEP: We have been walking since sunup.

BLACK FACE: I know where you are going. You are going toward the town. The little engine is there. You will see it. I want to see it again.

FIRST SHEEP: Why don't you come with us?

BLACK FACE: I can't get out. The gate is closed.

SECOND SHEEP: Good-by then. We'll tell the green engine we saw you.

[*The sheep move on, followed by the Shepherd with crook and pipe.*]

BLACK FACE: I want to go too. [*He pushes against the gate. The gate opens.*] Oh, the gate was not closed tightly. Now, I am free. I can find my little green engine. I'm coming. Wait for me. Wait! [*He romps off after the sheep.*]

## SCENE IV

*A business street in town. Late morning.*

SCENE: Several shopwindows are painted on the screen. The widest window belongs to a toy shop. In it stands a large woolly toy lamb.

[*A little girl enters, rolling a large hoop. A small dog frisks in, barking.*]

LITTLE GIRL: Come on, Spot.

SPOT: Bow-wow!

LITTLE GIRL: Jump through the hoop, Spot. Ready? One, two, three, jump! [*Spot jumps.*]

SPOT: Bow-wow-wow!

LITTLE GIRL: Good dog! Now again. Ready? One, two, three, jump!

[*Spot jumps through and runs out, followed by the Little Girl, just as the flock of sheep with the Shepherd come slowly in. Black Face is the last of the flock.*]

SHEPHERD: Keep together there—come now, keep together.

BLACK FACE [*explaining to his neighbor*]: This is the town—see all the houses and people.

FIRST SHEEP: It would be easy to get lost here.

BLACK FACE: Not for me. I know this town. [*Sees toy shop.*] What's that? A lamb in a glass house. [*He trots to the window.*]

SECOND SHEEP: Come, come, we shall be left behind.

BLACK FACE: No, I'm going to talk to the lamb. I want to ask him all about living in a glass house.

FIRST SHEEP: I am going to hurry.

SECOND SHEEP: You will be lost, Black Face—you'd better follow us.

[*They hurry out.*]

BLACK FACE [*tapping with his hoof against the toy-shop

*window*]: Hi, little lamb, why don't you look at me? Why don't you pay attention? I want to talk to you. Have you always lived in this glass house? Don't you ever come out to play? [*He taps again.*] Hi, hi! Silly lamb, why don't you talk? I wouldn't live in a glass house if it made me so stupid. [*He puts his forefeet on the ground and looks around. The flock is nowhere to be seen. Black Face runs back and forth looking for the flock.*] Where are the sheep? Where did they go? Down this way . . . No. This way . . . Oh no.

[*A little boy enters.*]

BOY: Come, Tom, here's a black-faced lamb.

[*Tom runs in.*]

TOM: Baa-baa, black sheep, have you any wool?

FIRST BOY: Yes sir; yes sir—three bags full.

BLACK FACE [*plaintively*]: Baa-aa!

TOM: I'll bet he's trying to talk to us.

FIRST BOY: Perhaps he is lost. Are you scared, little Black Face?

BLACK FACE: Baa-aa!

[*The Station Master strolls in.*]

STATION MASTER: Well, boys, what have you there?

BOTH BOYS [*together*]: A black-faced lamb, and we think he is lost.

STATION MASTER: He must belong to the flock of sheep that was on its way to the railway station. This is the second black-faced lamb lost in two days.

FIRST BOY: We can take him to the station, sir. We'll put him on the train with the other sheep.

STATION MASTER: You must hurry then. The train is just about to start.

TOM: Come, Black Face, come along.

BLACK FACE: Baa-baa!

[*Black Face and the boys hurry out.*]

## SCENE V

*In the meadow. Noon.*

[*Shepherdess sits sadly watching her sheep. Sheep bleat occasionally.*]

SHEPHERDESS: Poor little Black Face, where are you now? You were always so curious. Why were you so fond of the train? Now you have gone away with it. I fear that I shall never see you again.

[*Whistle of train is heard. As in Scene I the little train is seen as in the distance, then the larger train, and finally the full-sized train appears.*]

SHEPHERDESS: There is the noonday train now. I shall scold the Engineer for taking Black Face away. Stop! Stop!

[*She stands beside the fence and waves her crook as the full-sized train appears. Instead of a coach, there is a cattle car filled with sheep. Black Face is among them. The Shepherdess does not see him. The train has stopped.*]

SHEPHERDESS: Where is my lamb?

ENGINEER [*shaking his head*]: I don't know your lamb.

SHEPHERDESS: He climbed onto the track yesterday noon.

ENGINEER: Yes, I saw that lamb, but he jumped off into the ditch.

SHEPHERDESS: No, no, indeed he did not. He rode on the cowcatcher. I saw him with my very own eyes.

ENGINEER: Then he must have been the lost lamb on the station platform.

SHEPHERDESS: Poor Black Face!

ENGINEER: Sorry, miss. I don't know where he is now.

[*Engineer blows the whistle. Black Face has been trying to attract the Shepherdess's attention by bobbing up and down. As the train starts, he bleats loudly.*]

BLACK FACE: Baa-aa-aa!

SHEPHERDESS [*whirling around*]: There he is. Wait!
[*The train stops. The Engineer looks out of his cab again. The Shepherd gets out.*]

SHEPHERDESS [*to Shepherd*]: Did you have a black-faced lamb in your flock?

SHEPHERD: No, miss, the sheep I brought from the country this morning all had white faces. I don't know where this black-faced lamb came from.

SHEPHERDESS [*lifting Black Face out*]: Then he is mine.
[*Shepherdess pats his head. They stand together. Shepherdess waves as the train chugs away.*]

SHEPHERDESS: My foolish lamb, have you had enough traveling?

BLACK FACE: Baa-aa.

SHEPHERDESS [*putting her hand on his head*]: Be happy now in our green meadow. And when you tell the sheep about your adventures, be sure that you tell them how happy you are to be safely home at last.

A Group of Cut-out Shadow Plays Requiring Many Characters and More Difficult Handling:

THE TRAVELING MUSICIANS OF BREMEN
THE WOODEN HORSE
TOM, THE WATER BABY
DAVID COPPERFIELD

A group of seventh-grade children rehearsing the cut-out shadow play, "The Traveling Musicians of Bremen"

Two scenes from "The Traveling Musicians of Bremen"—a cut-out shadow play given by seventh-grade pupils

# THE TRAVELING MUSICIANS OF BREMEN

CHARACTERS: Donkey
Dog, Old Sport
Cock, Chanticleer
Cat, Old Mouser
First Robber, Tatters
Second Robber, Rags
Third Robber, Captain Buttons

## ACT I

*By the Roadside*

DONKEY [*enters left, sadly*]: Alas and alack, this is a sad day for me. I am old and weary. And to think of all the heavy loads I have carried for my master, and now he turns me out to die! What an ungrateful wretch he is. Fortunately I still have my wits and my beautiful musical voice. [*Brays.*] He-haw, he-haw. I'll go to Bremen and become the town musician. How now, who comes here? What a forlorn, sad-looking old dog!
[*Enter the Dog from the right.*]
What has happened to you, Old Sport? You look troubled, and you are all out of breath.

DOG: Enough has happened to me! I am old and tired and hungry, and I have come a long way. Because I am too old to hunt any longer, my master has forsaken me. Who will feed me now?

DONKEY: Cheer up, brother! I am going to Bremen to become the town musician. You had better join me, for I am sure you have a fine bass voice.

DOG: That I have! Bow-wow-wow. I shall be very glad to go with you.

DONKEY: Well, well, who is this looking as dismal as three wet days? What has happened to you, Old Mouser?

[*Enter the Cat from the right.*]

CAT: What has happened to me? All the misfortunes in the world. I am so old that my teeth are dull. I haven't caught a mouse in a month. My mistress wanted to drown me, so I ran away. Here I am, and what is to become of me?

DONKEY: Why, cheer up, old whiskers! Look at us! My master turned me out to die.

DOG: And my master was no better.

DONKEY: Are we downhearted? Not a bit of it. We are on our way to Bremen to become town musicians. Come and join us. You understand serenading, and we shall be glad of your company.

CAT: A very kind offer indeed. I'll begin to practice at once. Meouw, meouw.

[*Enter the Cock from right.*]

COCK [*flies up on a gate and begins to crow excitedly*]: Cock-a-doodle-do! Cock-a-doodle-do!

DONKEY: Stop, stop, your cries are enough to pierce bone and marrow. What is the matter?

COCK: The matter? The matter? Enough is the matter. My mistress told the cook to wring my neck; so I flew away, and here I am.

DONKEY: Hold on, Chanticleer. You have a fine shrill voice. Just what we need. We are going to Bremen to become town musicians. You had better join us.

COCK: I'll join you gladly. Cock-a-doodle-do. Cock-a-doodle-do.

DONKEY: What a fine company we are, and what a royal welcome awaits us in Bremen. Let us be on our way.

## ACT II

### Scene 1

*In the Woods*

TATTERS [*a robber with a pack on his back enters at left*]: Surely this is the place where those old rascals promised to meet me. Where are they, I'd like to know? [*He gives a long shrill whistle, which is answered by another whistle in the distance.*] That sounds like old Rags. I wonder what he's been up to. Here he comes, and it's high time too.
[*Enter Rags, from the left, without a pack.*]
Well, Rags, what luck today?

RAGS: Luck aplenty. If I hadn't had luck, I wouldn't be alive.

TATTERS [*disgusted*]: Where's your sack?

RAGS: That's where the luck came in.

TATTERS: What do you mean?

RAGS: I met the sheriff and his dog.

TATTERS: Well?

RAGS: When the dog jumped at me, I threw my sack at him and took to my heels.

TATTERS: A likely tale. Next you'll tell me the sack was full.

RAGS: And so it was, and a good haul too.

TATTERS: Tell that to Captain Buttons, you old fraud. [*Whistle in the distance. Tatters answers with a whistle.*] Wonder what luck he's had.
[*Enter Buttons from the left.*]

BUTTONS: Hello, Tatters and Rags. Hope you had as good a day as I've had. How about it?

TATTERS: Rags, tell him of your fine day.

RAGS: Just as I was on my way home, I met the sheriff——

BUTTONS: Ho, ho, just as usual, a fine robber you are.

Rags, look what I have, a feast for a week, a hen and a goose, a fine old cheese and good white bread. Now what do you say to getting home as fast as we can?

TATTERS AND RAGS: Hurrah! A feast, a feast!

[*Go off right, singing.*]

## ACT II

### Scene 2

*In the Woods*

DONKEY [*enters from left*]: Surely we have come a long way. [*Stops.*] But this seems a very safe and comfortable place to spend the night. Ho, comrades!

[*Enter the Dog from left.*]

Well, old comrade, what do you say to spending the night here?

DOG: Yes, yes, I'm ready to drop.

DONKEY: And where is Old Mouser?

CAT [*faintly*]: Meouw, meouw, meouw.

[*Enter the Cat from left.*]

DONKEY: Poor Old Mouser, lie down and rest.

[*Enter the Cock from left.*]

DONKEY: Come on, Brother Cock. There is a bed for you right up there on that high branch. Be sure to wake us in the morning. [*The Cock flies up on lowest branch of big tree.*]

COCK: What a dark night! [*Pause.*] What is that? A light?

DONKEY: Keep quiet up there. We want to sleep down here.

COCK: I see a light.

DONKEY: Keep still. It can't be a light.

COCK: But it is a light. A light in a house. I am certain.

DONKEY: Are you really certain?

COCK: Never more certain.

DONKEY: Well then, comrades. What do you say? Shall

we go and find out? Besides, these are very uncomfortable quarters.

DOG: Bow-wow. I can't sleep here.

CAT: Meouw, meouw, and I can't sleep here.

DONKEY: Come on, Brother Cock, and lead the way.

[*The Cock, the Dog, the Cat and the Donkey pass off the screen at right.*]

## ACT III

*The Robbers' House*

DONKEY [*enters left*]: Hush, hush, I'll go and look in the window.

DOG [*enters left*]: What do you see?

DONKEY: What do I see? I see a table spread with all sorts of good things to eat and to drink.

DOG: Do you see any meat?

CAT [*enters left*]: Do you see any milk?

COCK [*enters left*]: Do you see any corn?

DONKEY: Hush, hush. I see three robbers sitting at the table, just ready to eat.

COCK: That would just suit me.

CAT: Yes indeed, I wish that we were in their places.

DONKEY: Hush, hush, comrades. If we use our wits, we may yet sit in their places.

ALL: How? How?

DONKEY: I'll tell you. First I'll go up very quietly and put my front feet on the window sill; then, old-timer, you get up on my back. Now, Mouser, you jump up on Old-Timer's back; and, Cock, you fly up on Mouser's back; and when I count three, begin to sing. Now, ready.

DOG: All right.

CAT: Steady now.

COCK: Up I go.

DONKEY: Now then, one, two, three.

ALL TOGETHER {He-haw<br>Bow-wow<br>Meouw<br>Cock-a-doodle-do

[*They burst through the window; and the robbers run wildly out of the house to the right while the animals take their places at the table.*]

DONKEY: Well done, brothers. Didn't I tell you if we used our wits we could frighten them away?

DOG: Yes, yes, but I'm too hungry to talk. Give me a bone.

CAT: Give me the cream. Give me the cream.

COCK: This is all right for me. This is all right for me.

DONKEY: Never had such a feast in my life. Never had such a feast in my life. What say you to staying here for the rest of our lives?

ALL {Fine!<br>Couldn't be better!<br>It satisfies me!

DONKEY: Agreed then, comrades, and now to bed.

[(*Dim the light by covering light with blue tissue paper, thin blue cloth or light-weight paper.*) *The Cat jumps up on the table and goes to sleep. The Dog lies down inside the house near the window. The Cock flies out the window and up on the roof to sleep. The Donkey goes out the window and lies down in the yard. The robbers come sneaking back at left.*]

THE CAPTAIN: The light is out, and it's all quiet.

FIRST ROBBER: They have gone away.

SECOND ROBBER: I'm terribly hungry.

THE CAPTAIN: Here, old fellow, you go into the house and see if all is well.

FIRST ROBBER: Why don't you all come?

THE CAPTAIN: Do as I tell you.

[*First Robber goes into the house through the window and over to the table. Now the Cat scratches him. He screams and jumps out through the window.*

*The Dog bites him in the leg, and he howls. As he runs through the yard, the Donkey kicks him, and he moans.*]

COCK [*crows*]: Hurrah, throw him up to me! Hurrah, throw him up to me!

SECOND ROBBER: Captain, Captain, run for your life! This place is full of witches and demons. Run, run for your life.

CAT: After the scratches I gave, they'll never come back.

DOG: After the bites I gave, they'll never come back.

COCK: Cock-a-doodle-do! We will live here in peace for the rest of our lives.

DONKEY: You have certainly done well, my comrades. Now I think that Bremen town will have to get along without our music. What do you say to singing a song? Let's call it "The Robbers' Farewell." One, two, three.

[*All the animals singing together*] {He haw<br>Meouw, meouw<br>Bow-wow<br>Cock-a-doodle-do.

## THE WOODEN HORSE

or *The Siege of Troy*

CHARACTERS APPEARING IN THIS PLAY:

Homer (Hom-er), a great Greek poet, who was blind, and lived about 1000 B.C.

Odysseus (O-dis-us), King of Ithaca.

Agamemnon (Aga-mem-non), King of Mycenae.

Menelaus (Men-e-la-us), King of Sparta and brother of Agamemnon.

Helen (Hel-en), wife of Menelaus, who was later spoken of as Helen of Troy.

Klymene (Klime-ne), handmaiden of Helen of Troy.

Athene (A-the-ne), Goddess of Wisdom.

Greek captains and soldiers.

Trojan captains and soldiers.

CHARACTERS MENTIONED IN THIS PLAY:

Priam (Pri-am), King of Troy.

Hector (Hec-tor) and Paris (Par-is), sons of King Priam.

Achilles (A-kil-ez), a Greek hero.

Clytaemnestra (Klit-em-nes-tra), wife of Agamemnon.

Philocklas (Phi-lock-las), a Greek hero.

Penelope (Pe-nel-o-pe), wife of Odysseus.

Telemachus (Te-lem-a-kus), son of Odysseus and Penelope.

Hera (He-ra), wife of Zeus (Zus).

Aphrodite (Af-ro-di-te), Goddess of Beauty.

Poseidon (Po-si-don), God of the Sea.

"The Traveling Musicians of Bremen"

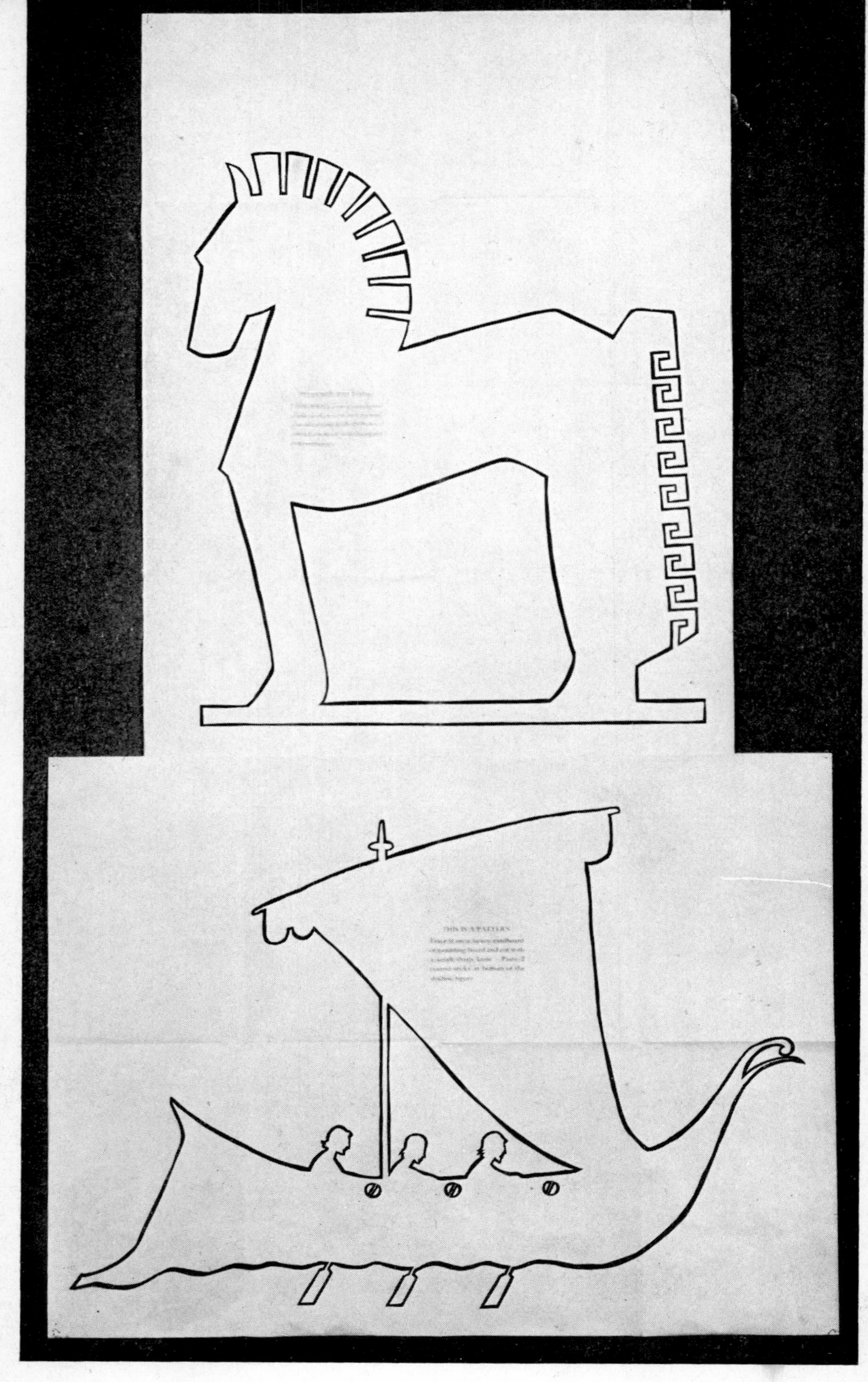

Drawings for the wooden horse and one of the ships in the cut-out shadow play, "The Wooden Horse"

## CUT–OUT SHADOW PLAYS

PROLOGUE: The blind poet, Homer, sitting in the market place of a Greek city, tells his countrymen the story of how the Trojan War began.

ACT I: On the Greek ships lying off the coast of Troy.
ACT II: SCENE 1. Inside the walls of Troy.
SCENE 2. Same.
ACT III: The Greek ships sail homeward.

EPILOGUE: Homer, again sitting in the market place of a Greek city, tells of the return of Odysseus and other Greek warriors to their native lands.

## PROLOGUE

*In the Market Place*

[*This part of the play may be read or spoken, just as the actors prefer, either in front of or behind the shadow screen.*]

HOMER [*leaning forward and speaking earnestly, as though continuing a story*]: Now, my friends, you have heard of Paris, the son of King Priam, and of how it was foretold that he would bring death and destruction on the fair city of Troy. You have also heard of how Paris was sent from his father's house to live with the shepherds on Mount Ida, and of how he was called upon to decide which of three Goddesses was the most beautiful, Hera, Athene or Aphrodite. Aphrodite, you remember, promised him the fairest of all women for his wife if he would decide in her favor. This fairest of all women was none other than Helen, the wife of Menelaus, King of Sparta. When Paris came to Sparta and stole this fair Helen, King Menelaus called upon his brother Agamemnon and the other kings of Greece to make war upon the Trojans and to help him to recover his wife.

After much preparation, they sailed forth in their swift ships attended by many brave men. For nine long years they lay siege to the great walled city of Troy.

I have told you ofttimes of the many battles fought on the plain before those mighty walls between the Greeks and Trojans and of the woes innumerable that came upon them. Finally, sick at heart, they knew not what to do. Now you shall hear how crafty Odysseus saved his comrades.

## ACT I

### *The Sea*

TIME: Nine years after the Greek heroes left their homes in Greece. The Greek ships are lying off the coast of Troy.

[*One ship is sailing in the middle of the screen. One ship is departing, and one ship is just arriving.*]

FIRST WARRIOR [*standing on middle ship and sadly lifting his hand*]: There still stand the great walls of Troy.

SECOND WARRIOR [*standing near by, speaks hopelessly*]: After all our efforts of nine long years, those walls still defy us. I cannot endure it.

FIRST WARRIOR [*sadly*]: Hundreds of our brave comrades have fallen there on that plain before those mighty walls.

SECOND WARRIOR: And now the plague is upon us and has smitten more men than even the Trojans have killed.

FIRST WARRIOR: And where, pray tell me, are all the riches and glory that we promised ourselves?

SECOND WARRIOR: And what, pray tell me, comrade, is happening to our wives and children at home?

FIRST WARRIOR [*hopelessly*]: May the Gods protect them.

SECOND WARRIOR: And what lies before us here?

FIRST WARRIOR: Sorrow and defeat. The Trojans will burn our ships and drive us into the sea.

SECOND WARRIOR: But we have made a vow to the immortal Gods and must fight on.

FIRST WARRIOR: Yes, and we still have brave men with us, although mighty Achilles is no more.

SECOND WARRIOR: Odysseus is valiant and cunning. Thanks be to Athene, he is still among the living.

FIRST WARRIOR: Surely he must have some plan to save us.

SECOND WARRIOR [*calling loudly*]: Odysseus, Odysseus, Odysseus!

ODYSSEUS [*as his ship draws near from left*]: Who calls?

FIRST WARRIOR: Your comrades call you, great Odysseus. Our spirits can no longer bear these terrible misfortunes.

SECOND WARRIOR: Will there be no end to this struggle?

ODYSSEUS [*confidently*]: Their walls may be mighty, but by the help of the immortal Gods, we'll outwit those Trojans yet.

FIRST WARRIOR [*eagerly*]: But tell us, crafty Odysseus, what is your plan?

ODYSSEUS: Give ear, my friends. What say you to building a great wooden horse, large enough to conceal a company of our bravest warriors?

SECOND WARRIOR: Where could you build such a great horse, mighty Odysseus?

ODYSSEUS [*motioning to the right*]: Out there on the plain, before their very eyes.

FIRST WARRIOR [*troubled*]: But the Trojans will see us.

ODYSSEUS: I want them to see us. After we have built it, we will burn our stores and pretend to sail away.

FIRST WARRIOR [*still unconvinced*]: What, leave our best warriors imprisoned in the great horse?

ODYSSEUS: Listen well. We will leave a spy behind us, who with cunning and deceit will pretend that he is a deserter from our ranks. He will tell the Trojans that the wooden horse is an offering to Pallas Athene for a safe return to our homes.

SECOND WARRIOR [*eagerly*]: And what then?

ODYSSEUS: I feel certain that the Trojans will try to win the favor of the Goddess by taking the horse into their city.

FIRST WARRIOR: But such a horse as you describe, brave Odysseus, could not pass through the gates.

ODYSSEUS: Have no fears, comrades. The Trojans will tear down their mighty walls to win the favor of Pallas Athene. After they take the wooden horse within their walls, our spy will light a signal so that we may return and destroy their city.

SECOND WARRIOR [*interrupting*]: Steal into the city and take the Trojans by surprise!

FIRST WARRIOR: A worthy plan, Odysseus. Pallas Athene herself will direct us.

ODYSSEUS: Now let us take food and rest. Tomorrow at daybreak we go ashore and begin to build the wooden horse.

FIRST AND SECOND WARRIORS: May the Gods be with us. [*Pallas Athene appears in the distance, walking with uplifted arm, on the waters, but she is not seen by the heroes.*]

## ACT II

### Scene I

*Inside the Walls of Troy*

TIME: Early morning.

FIRST TROJAN SENTINEL [*stands on wall at top of stairs, lifts arm to head as though trying to see more clearly*]: What do I see emerging from yonder mists? Can it be that the Greeks are departing?

SECOND TROJAN SENTINEL: And the great wooden horse, do you think that they have finished it?

FIRST TROJAN SENTINEL [*excitedly*]: Call our comrades. Call our comrades.

SECOND SENTINEL [*calling*]: Up, up, comrades. See, see the Greeks.

FIRST SENTINEL: And what fires are those I see there? Surely not watch fires. I know their campfires well.

TROJAN WARRIOR: Look, look, they haul their stores and throw them on the flames.

FIRST SENTINEL: What means all this?

SECOND SENTINEL: Look again. They set their sails.

TROJAN WARRIOR: And they are deserting the great wooden horse. Look, they leave their fires and take to their ships.

FIRST SENTINEL: Run, run, spread the news. Tell King Priam.

SECOND SENTINEL: What do you think all this means, comrade?

FIRST SENTINEL: It's plain enough. They are defeated at last. Our heroes and our God-made walls are unconquerable.

SECOND SENTINEL: It may well be so. They are weary, I know, and their losses have been very great.

FIRST SENTINEL: They are heartsick for their homes.

SECOND SENTINEL: But why did they build the wooden horse, working long days when the sun was white upon the plain?

FIRST SENTINEL: Could it be an offering to their gods?

SECOND SENTINEL: But still I cannot see why they would build a wooden horse as an offering.

WARRIORS [*entering at right*]: Look, look. The wind fills their sails; they move, they move! The Greeks are defeated at last. All glory to the Trojans. The Gods are with us. [*Enter Greek Spy, pretending to be a fugitive.*]

GREEK SPY: Alas, where is there a spot on earth or sea

that will give me shelter now? Every hand is against me, crying for bloody vengeance.

FIRST CAPTAIN: Not so, wretch. Speak! We will listen.

SPY: Ah, my lords, I will tell you truly. I will not deny that I am a Greek by birth, but having brought down upon myself the jealousy of Odysseus, my ruin began. He threatened me until my life became unbearable. Last night I escaped him and made my way hither. Now I throw myself upon your mercy.

CAPTAIN [*sternly*]: Only the King can grant you mercy. But tell us, before you go, what means that great wooden horse?

SPY [*with great pretense*]: Worthy Captain, it is an offering to the Goddess, Pallas Athene. The Greeks seek her favor against their safe and speedy return to their homes.

FIRST CAPTAIN [*commanding*]: Soldiers, take this fugitive to King Priam and let him tell his tale.

SECOND CAPTAIN: I have a crafty idea. Let us bring this wooden horse within our walls.

FIRST CAPTAIN: What strange madness is this, my countrymen? Think you that the enemy has sailed away or that a Greek could ever make a gift that had no treachery in it? It is too large to bring within our walls.

SECOND CAPTAIN [*persistently*]: Then let us tear down a part of the wall.

FIRST CAPTAIN: No, never. These mighty walls have protected us for nine long years. They shall not be broken.

SECOND CAPTAIN: But it is an offering to Pallas Athene herself. It is well to win her favor.

FIRST CAPTAIN: Her favor has long been with the Greeks. I like it not, men of Troy, and I beg of you to put no faith in this horse. I fear a Greek even with a gift in his hand.

SECOND CAPTAIN: What say you all? Shall we bring this

great wooden horse within our walls and win the favor of the fair Goddess Athene? Here comes a messenger from the King. What says King Priam?

MESSENGER: The King commands, bring in the great wooden horse.

ALL [*in chorus, shouting*]: Bring it in, yes, bring it in. Bring in the great wooden horse. Tear down the walls. Bring in the great wooden horse.

THIRD CAPTAIN: Bring on the battering rams.

FIRST CAPTAIN: I like it not. We shall pay for this.

[*Sounds of falling masonry, pounding and cheering; many figures cross the scene from low to high part of wall.*]

SECOND CAPTAIN [*excitedly*]: See how the great stones fall, Pallas Athene. We do this in thy honor.

WARRIOR: A break in the great wall. Clear the way.

SECOND CAPTAIN [*shouting*]: Clear the way. They are bringing in the great horse.

FIRST CAPTAIN [*sadly*]: I like it not.

[*As the horse is pulled in, the Trojan warriors stand with raised spears and shout.*]

TROJAN WARRIORS [*shouting*]: Hail to Athene. Hail to Athene. Honor and renown to the conquering Trojans.

[*Lights go out.*]

## ACT II

### Scene 2

*Inside the Walls of Troy*

TIME: Night (change white bulb to blue or cover white bulb with blue tissue paper).

[*Enter Helen of Troy from left.*]

HELEN OF TROY [*walking about*]: So great a horse was never seen before this hour. It is the work of my countrymen. [*Drawing near the horse.*] There is space within for many men. If there are men within, they are Greek heroes who have come to rescue me from the Trojans, me, Helen—wife of Menelaus, who was stolen by Paris these many years ago. [*Thoughtfully.*] Odysseus is clever, but I think I know a way to discover his plan. I shall call each hero in the voice of his wife. If he is within, he will surely answer. [*Sweetly.*] Philocklas, Philocklas. I am thy wife, weary with waiting. Speak to me. Come to me. [*Silence.*] He does not answer. [*Calling again.*] Odysseus, great Odysseus, wise above all men. Have you forgotten your wife, Penelope? I am weary for sight of thee. Speak to me. [*Silence. Calling again most sweetly.*] Menelaus, Menelaus, my dear husband. I am thy wife Helen. I call upon thee. If within this great horse, come out to me. Menelaus. Menelaus. [*Silence. Sadly.*] Strange it is that no man answers. Yet I have a feeling that Greek heroes are near at hand. [*Helen goes out to the right, and at the extreme right a red signal light is seen upon the plain without the wall. A tiny red bulb may be flashed off and on several times on the right. Figures now are seen stealing from the wooden horse; stage almost dark.*]

ODYSSEUS [*in a low voice*]: The plan has worked. The signal fires bring back our men. The time draws near for the attack.

MENELAUS: May the immortal Gods give us strength and courage.

AGAMEMNON: This is our last stand. If we fail tonight, we are conquered.

ODYSSEUS [*firmly*]: We shall not fail. Our men are here. Courage, Menelaus, Helen shall be ours before the dawn.

MENELAUS: May the Gods grant it.

[*The Greek warriors arrive, and in the confusion one hears deep low voices calling, "Odysseus, Mene-*

*laus, we have come. Lead on, lead on. Down with the Trojans." Loud cries in the distance as Trojan warriors shout, "The Greeks, the Greeks. The Greeks are upon us. The horse was a trap." Fighting goes on around the horse, much confusion and shouting. Now the Greek warriors shout, "Down with the Trojans. Fight on, or we are conquered. We are winning. We win. We win. Helen is ours at last." Dayight breaks. (Take away blue paper, or if blue bulb has been used, turn on flashlight close to blue bulb, then turn out blue bulb.) The Trojans' dead are lying on the ground while the Greek warriors stand about and shout.]*

ODYSSEUS [*commanding*]: Menelaus, lead fair Helen to the ships. Fill them with treasures, my brave comrades, and we shall set out for our homes. Lead on, Menelaus, and may Athene grant us a safe voyage.

## ACT III

*The Sea*

The Greek ships sail homeward.
TIME: Night.

KLYMENE [*coming up to Helen, who appears to be seated in the prow of the ship*]: Are you asleep, fair Helen? Why do you sit here alone?

HELEN OF TROY: Ah, gentle Klymene, the beauty of the night stirs my heart with gentle memories.

KLYMENE: Does not your heart rejoice that we are now about to turn our faces homeward?

HELEN OF TROY: Yes, I, too, feel drawn to our dear homeland. As our ships turn their prows to the blue sea, I ease my heart with a sigh. May I again see my loved ones.

KLYMENE: Sweet mistress, may the Gods, who live at ease, never again leave you to weep and pine.

HELEN OF TROY [*tenderly*]: Of noble blood you are, dear maid, you who have followed me these many long years and tended my every need.

KLYMENE: How gladly I have served you, fair Helen, through all the years of our wandering, and through these nine years of our stay here in Troy.

HELEN OF TROY: Among my treasures that fill this ship there is a well-wrought bowl of silver. Its rim is finished with gold. It is of all my treasures the most precious to me. Take it. I gladly give it thee.

KLYMENE: I am not worthy of so fair a gift.

HELEN OF TROY: Take it, and may it bring thee many happy memories. [*Exit Klymene. Helen of Troy again sits alone. Menelaus approaches Helen from the right. Helen then rises and walks very slowly toward Menelaus.*]

MENELAUS: Take heart, fair Helen, and be not troubled. A true guide goes with us. Powerful she is, for it is none other than Pallas Athene herself. Seeing you grieve, she pities you, and it was she who sent me here to tell you so.

HELEN OF TROY: My noble husband, favored of the Gods, my soul is glad that you are come, Menelaus.

MENELAUS: For your sake I have, in days gone by, tested the wisdom and the will of many heroes, and I have traveled over many lands.

HELEN OF TROY: I grieve, not for myself alone, but for those who fell on the plain of Troy.

MENELAUS: For them, too, I often grieve and mourn, but most for you, dear wife, stolen from your home and made to wander and dwell with strangers.

HELEN OF TROY: Nor do I grieve for my countrymen alone, but also for the Trojan heroes whom I came to know so well. Chief among them noble Hector, Priam's son. Never heard I evil or despiteful word from him. When others upbraided me, he comforted me with gentle kindly words.

MENELAUS: That can I well believe, for he was a noble foe.

HELEN OF TROY: Nor can I ever forget the kindness of that great King, Priam, his father, who never blamed me, the cause of all of his sorrows.

MENELAUS: Yes, my dear wife, your grief I feel. May the Gods who have protected us in battle and given us victory still protect us on our voyage.

HELEN OF TROY: A ship approaches.

[*Agamemnon's ship draws up from right.*]

MENELAUS: Hail, Agamemnon. May the Gods give wind to your sails and bring you swiftly to your native land. We shall soon follow you over the sacred sea. Farewell.

AGAMEMNON [*calling as his ship passes from right to left*]: A good voyage, brother. Farewell! Farewell!

[*Odysseus' ship now draws up from right to left.*]

ODYSSEUS [*calls out*]: Hail, Menelaus. Hail, fair Helen. Our sails are set for Ithaca. If earth-shaking Poseidon wills it, the sea will bear me swiftly home to my dear wife, Penelope, and our fair son, Telemachus. But if he wreck me on a surging sea, I will be patient still, bearing within my breast a heart well tried with trouble.

MENELAUS: It is true, mighty Odysseus, in times past much have we borne and much have we toiled in waves and war.

HELEN OF TROY: Surely the immortal Gods must grant good fortune to your wearied souls.

MENELAUS: I feel that bright-eyed Athene will protect us.

ODYSSEUS: Even now she seems near. [*Calls to his men in the ships.*] Spread forth the sails, in all ships. Let the wind carry us homeward.

[*Chorus of men in all the ships*]: Ai, Ai, Ai, Ai.

[*In the distance Athene is seen walking slowly over the water, with upraised arm, as the ships move off left.*]

## EPILOGUE

*In the Market Place*

[*Homer sitting in the market place as in Prologue. These lines may be read or spoken in front of scenery or back of scenery.*]

HOMER: And now, my friends, the siege of Troy is over. We have seen the brave Greeks take to their good ships and turn their faces homeward. Good fortune and favoring winds followed them. But alas, not so for mighty Odysseus. Shortly after leaving Troy he offended Poseidon, the God of the Sea, and for this offense he was doomed to wander still another ten years, his good ships wrecked, his men all lost and near to death he came. At last the Gods relented and brought him to his home and his faithful wife, Penelope, and his son, Telemachus, now grown to manhood.

When we meet here again in this fair porch, I will relate, if you wish to hear, all the adventures of that great wanderer, mighty Odysseus.

## TOM, THE WATER BABY

A Dramatization of Charles Kingsley's novel *The Water Babies.*

TIME: Nineteenth century.
PLACE: England.

CHARACTERS:

Tom
Grimes
Rabbit
Keeper
Ellie
Old Nurse
Old Dame
Big Trout
Two Small Trout
Two Caddises
Dragonfly
Insect
Otter
Salmon
Sunfish
Five Sea Snails
Lobster
First Water Baby
Second Water Baby
Mrs. Doasyouwouldbedoneby
Mrs. Bedonebyasyoudid
Truncheon
Blunderbuss

PROLOGUE: Before the gates of Harthover Place.

ACT I: SCENE 1. Ellie's bedroom.
SCENE 2. At the foot of Lewthwaite Crag.
ACT II: Below the river bank.
ACT III: Under the sea.
ACT IV: The Other End of Nowhere.

### PROLOGUE

[*Before the gates of Harthover Place. The great wrought-iron gates are closed, and above the high walls can be seen the roof of the keeper's house and the thick foliage of large trees. A bench is set against the wall at the left of the gate. It is an early morning in spring.*]

[*A gruff, surly voice off stage*]: Hi, ye young jackanapes, come along. The likes of thee picking flowers! Get along.

[*Grimes enters from left, riding a donkey. He is a big, burly, coarse man.*]

Hoa!

[*Tom, a dirty little chimney sweep, who has never washed himself and has never been taught to say his prayers, who has been used to being hungry and being beaten, but who laughs when he has a chance and takes a lively interest in everything about him, walks slowly after his master, two big brooms over his shoulder.*]

GRIMES: Hoa! Well, here we be, and it's a hard road to come over at three o'clock in the morning. I near fell off the donkey to get a bit of a nap. Hi there, Tom, what are you looking at?

TOM [*with awe*]: Master, it's a grand place we've come to, ain't it?

GRIMES: Right thou art, boy, no grander place the country round than Harthover, and Sir John's the grand old man, I'm telling ye. Harthover Place is that old, nobody knows how old. And fur chimneys there 're so many ye'd best be taking a care that ye don't get lost in 'em and never get down. Now pull the gate bell, boy, and no more talk. Ha, what's that?

[*A rabbit hops across the stage.*]

TOM: Oh, Master, what was the creature?

GRIMES: Mind thy head, Tom, and pull the bell. While thou art up chimneys, I'll have a game of my own, I'm thinking.

GATE KEEPER [*opens the gates and comes out*]: Well,

Grimes, I was told to expect thee. Now thou 'lt be so good as to keep to the main avenue, and not let me find a hare or a rabbit on thee when thou comest back. I shall look sharp for one, I tell thee.

GRIMES [*laughing*]: Not if it's in the bottom of the soot bag.

GATE KEEPER [*laughing*]: If that's thy sort, I may as well walk up with thee to the hall.

GRIMES [*sitting down on the bench*]: And a little rest a man needs before he starts up that way.

GATE KEEPER: Ye are a lazy fellow. Ye rode all the way, and the lad walked and carried the brooms too, I'll wager.

GRIMES: And what would ye—have the master walk and the sweep ride? [*Laughs carelessly.*]

TOM: What's that sound, sir, that goes biz-z-z-z-z?

GATE KEEPER: The bees about the lime flowers.

TOM: What are bees?

GATE KEEPER: What make honey.

TOM: What is honey?

GRIMES: Thou hold thy noise!

GATE KEEPER: Let the boy be. He's a civil young chap now, and that's more than he'll be long if he bides with thee.

GRIMES [*gives a snort*]: Ho, ho.

TOM: I wish I was a keeper, to live in such a beautiful place, and wear green velveteens, and have a real dog whistle at my button, like you.

GATE KEEPER: Let well enough alone, lad, and ill too, at times. Thou canst drink at the spring before going up to the hall. Art thou thirsty?

TOM: Yes sir. My master dipped his head in a spring by the roadside. I never saw him do that before.

GRIMES: Nor will again, most likely. 'Twasn't for cleanliness I did it, but for coolness. I'd be ashamed to want washing every week or so, like any smutty collier lad.

TOM: I wanted to dip my head in. It would be as good as putting it under the town pump, and there was no beadle to drive a chap away.

GRIMES: Thou stop thy noise. What dost want with washing thyself? Thou didst not drink half a gallon of beer last night, like me.

GATE KEEPER: Well, Grimes, thou had best be moving if the lad is to sweep out the chimneys this day.

GRIMES: Mind that, you young beggar, and move along. Now then, Bess, my girl. [*Takes hold of donkey's rein.*] Not so fast, Master Keeper—I'm a heavy man.

## ACT I

[SCENE I. *Ellie's bedroom. A pretty room all white and rose. There is a fireplace in the middle of the back wall. Ellie's bed is in the left corner. Casement windows in the right wall, opening outward, give a glimpse of blue sky and sunlit trees. There is a washing stand on which are bowl, pitcher, towels, etc., a small table on which are some flowers, a little seat by the fire, fire irons against the fireplace, and a coal pail. Ellie, a lovely little girl with golden curls, is lying in bed asleep. The stout old nurse comes in, goes to the casement windows and throws them wide open.*]

NURSE: Welladay, how the pretty dear sleeps.

ELLIE [*stirs and calls sleepily*]: Nurse dear, is it a nice day?

NURSE: As nice a day as a child could wish. Not a cloud in the sky. A fine day for the hunt. Thy father will be up and over the hills, I'll wager, long e'er this.

ELLIE: The poor fox, Nurse. The poor little red fox. I hope it gets away from the cruel dogs.

NURSE: Little chance of that, but I pray they never chase another one into the conservatory. Such a hubbub there was before the dogs caught it. Such a breaking of glass and smashing of flower pots. Such a noise, hubbub and hullabaloo was ne'er heard before.

ELLIE: And the poor fox, Nurse. How frightened it must have been.

NURSE: Lord bless the child's tender heart. Now, my precious, just lie thee down and take a nap till the bath water is hot. There now. [*She gives Ellie an affectionate pat and goes out at left.*]

ELLIE [*happily*]: Oh, it's the month of May, the month of May—and the flowers are blooming everywhere.

NURSE [*outside*]: Take a nap, my precious.

[*Ellie lies quietly on her pillow. Tom comes down the chimney and stands on the hearth. He looks like a little black ape.*]

TOM: I'm lost, that's what I am, and my eyes are full of soot. My, what a pretty room. Not a speck of dirt anywhere—not a bit of soot. [*He sees Ellie.*] Oh my! I wonder if she could ever have been dirty. Are all people like that when they are washed? I'd like to be clean. I'm only a black dirty chimney sweep, but I'd like to be clean. [*He looks at his hands and begins to cry.*] If [*sobs*] I [*sob*] washed hard——

[*He stumbles and hits the fire tongs, which fall against the coal pail with a clatter. Ellie jumps up in bed and on seeing Tom screams.*]

NURSE [*comes running in from left, sees Tom and tries to grab him, calling out*]: Help, fire, murder, help! [*Tom pulls away from her and jumps out the window. Ellie jumps out of bed and runs to the window, the nurse leaves the room (right) calling, "Help, thief, stop, thief, help!"*]

ELLIE [*looking out of the window*]: There he goes across the lawn and over the iron railings, and there goes the gardener after him, and the dairy maid, too, and the steward, and the groom, and the keeper, and [*she turns around*] he really didn't do anything but frighten me. He was so black! He is a chimney sweep, I suppose. Perhaps he got lost in the chimneys. He didn't steal anything. Perhaps he was frightened too—and now everyone is chasing him. Oh dear, oh dear, I hope no one catches him. He is only a poor little, dirty chimney sweep.

[SCENE 2. *At the foot of Lewthwaite Crag. The back wall represents a steep, gray stone crag with jutting ledges, green-stalked ferns grow at its base, silver-backed leaves hang over the ledges, rock roses and saxifrage grow in the rocky crevices. At the left of the stage is the front of a neat little cottage. A clipped yew hedge encloses the garden at the right; there is a swinging gate; the garden is full of bright-colored flowers. Tom is first seen high up on the crag. He lets himself down from ledge to ledge. Halfway down he rests.*]

TOM: I can stop and rest a bit now. No one can get me here. The world looked a big place from the top of yon crag. I'm that hot, I'm burning up, and it must be Sunday, for I can hear church bells ringing a long way off.

[*He climbs down into the garden and goes toward the cottage door. Before he reaches it, the nicest old woman comes to the door. She wears a red petticoat, short dimity bedgown and clean white cap, with a black silk handkerchief over it, tied under her chin.*]

OLD DAME: What art thou, and what dost want? A chimney sweep! Away with thee! I'll have no sweeps here.

TOM: Water.

OLD DAME: Water? There's plenty in the river.

TOM: But I can't get there; I'm most clemmed with hunger and drought. [*He sinks down on the doorstep.*]

OLD DAME: He's sick, and a bairn's a bairn, sweep or none.

TOM: Water.

OLD DAME: God forgive me! Water's bad for thee. I'll give thee milk. [*She goes indoors and returns with a cup of milk which she holds to Tom's lips.*] Where didst come from?

TOM: Over Fell there [*pointing up to the crag*].

OLD DAME: Over Harthover? And down Lewthwaite Crag? Art sure thou art not lying?

TOM: Why should I?

OLD DAME: How got ye up there?

TOM: I came over from the Place. My master Grimes sent me up the chimneys, and I got lost—and they took me for a thief and everyone chased me. I never stopped running till I came to the crag.

OLD DAME: Bless thy little heart! And thou hast not been stealing, then?

TOM: No. [*Leans his head wearily against the door.*]

OLD DAME: Bless thy little heart! And I'll warrant not. Why God's guided the bairn because he was innocent! Away from the Place, and over Harthover, and down Lewthwaite Crag! Who ever heard the like if God hadn't led him? Wilt have some bread?

TOM: I can't.

OLD DAME: It's good enough, for I made it myself.

TOM: I can't. [*Pause.*] Is it Sunday?

OLD DAME: No then, why should it be?

TOM: Because I hear the church bells ringing so.

OLD DAME: Bless thy pretty heart! The bairn's sick. Come wi' me. If thou wert a bit cleaner, I'd put thee in my own bed for the Lord's sake. But come along here. Lie thee down on this old rug and sleep away thy giddiness, and in an hour's time I will come out. [*Tom lies down. The good Dame goes into the house, but Tom can't lie still. He moves about and begins to talk.*]

TOM: The church bells keep on ringing. I'm too dirty to go into a church. [*His voice sounds as if he were talking in a dream.*] I must be clean, I must be clean. I must go to the river and wash. Oh, I must be quick and wash myself. [*He sits up.*] The bells are ringing quite loud now, and they will stop soon, and then the door will be shut, and I shall never be able to get in at all. [*He gets up and goes toward the gate.*] I shall go to the river. It is cool, cool, cool. I will be a fish. I will swim in the water. I must be clean, I must be clean.

[*He goes out through the gate.*]

## ACT II

[*Below the riverbank. The backdrop represents a rocky bank with jutting ledges, water plants of various kinds growing in the crevices and up from the river bottom. There are several large rocks on the stage, and near the front more water plants and small rocks. When the curtains open, the scene is flooded with a dim bluish-green light, the rushes are waving, and dimly seen forms are swimming about.*]

[*Sweet childish voices off stage, calling*]: Oh, Fairy Queen, oh, Fairy Queen, where have you been, where have you been?

VOICE OF QUEEN: I have been smoothing sick folks' pillows, and whispering sweet dreams into their ears: coaxing little children away from the gutters and from foul places. Doing all I can to help those who cannot help themselves. And I have brought you a new little brother and watched him safe all the way.

WATER BABIES: A new water baby? Where is he? Oh, where?

VOICE OF QUEEN: No, children, he must not see you or know that you are here. He is but a little savage now, and like the beasts that perish; and from the beasts that perish he must learn. So you must not play with him, or speak to him, or let him see you: but only keep him from being harmed.

WATER BABIES: We shall keep him from being harmed.

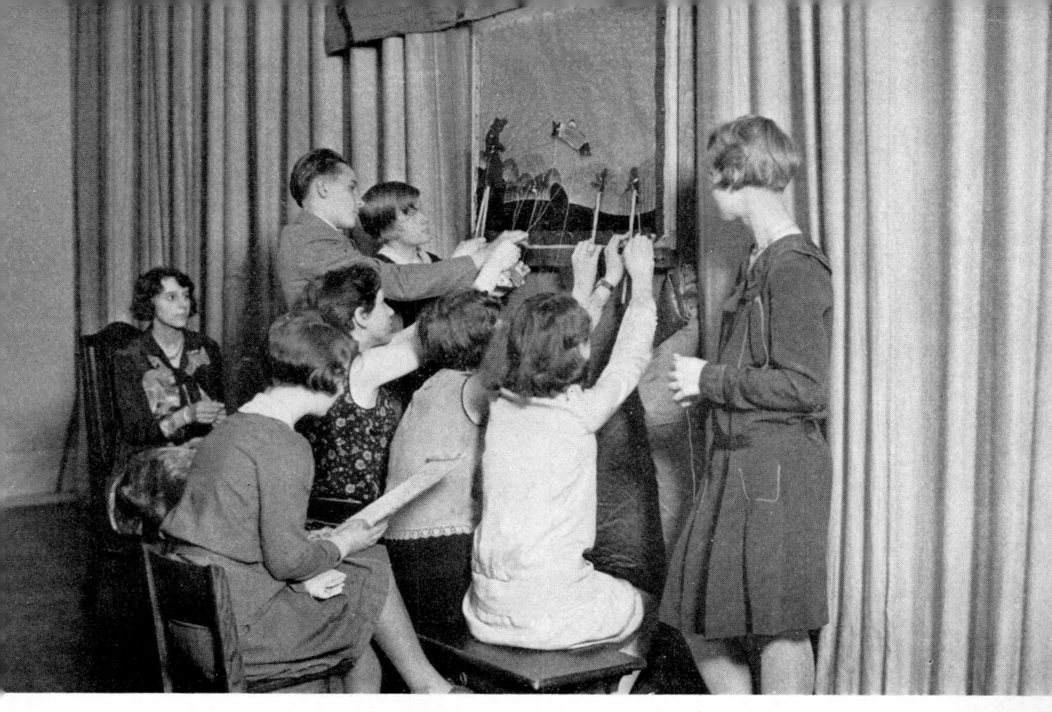

Rehearsal for "Tom, the Water Baby," a cut-out shadow play given by a group of ninth-grade pupils

Prologue for "Tom, the Water Baby," the great hall, trees and walls were printed on the screen in color and do not appear when photographed

ACT I, *Scene* 1, Ellie's Bedroom—from the shadow play, "Tom, the Water Baby"

*Scene* 2, At the foot of Lewthwaite Crag

[*Their voices fade away in the distance.*] We shall keep him from being harmed. [*The light grows stronger, and amber rays of sunshine slant downward through the waving plants and rushes. Tom, now a beautiful little water baby with a lacy frill of gills around his neck, gets up from a bed of soft rushes where he has been lying asleep. He has completely forgotten that he ever was a dirty little chimney sweep. A full-grown trout and two young ones go swimming by.*]

TOM: Oh, you pretty things. Stop! Wait! Come play with me.

[*The big trout swims away, but the little ones swim around Tom. They are as big as he is.*]

I'll catch you. Swim—swim.

TROUT: No, you can't. We'll hide. [*They go behind the rushes.*]

TOM: Come out. Come out.

TROUT: Here we come. Run—run, run. [*They chase Tom.*] Away we go to catch flies for supper—green ones, black ones and nice big blue ones. Good-by.

TOM: Good-by. [*He goes to the large rock at left of stage and calls.*] Come out, come out, Caddises, and play with me.

CADDISES: We haven't time for play. You are only a silly little water baby, but we are ladies of fashion. We are busy all day long dressing ourselves up [*they come out*] with pebbles and wood and bits of shell.

FIRST CADDIS [*she has a long straw for a tail*]: Hurrah! My sister down the river has a tail, and I'll have one too. We are ladies of fashion We shall walk along the riverbank in our fine new clothes.

[*They go out right.*]

TOM [*laughing*]: You are funny, but you don't know how funny you are.

[*He turns to the rock at the right, and a creature larger than Tom comes out. It is ugly and dirty-*

*looking, with six legs and a big stomach and a ridiculous head with two great eyes and a face like a donkey's. Tom jumps up and down in front of it.*]
Oh! you are an ugly fellow, to be sure! Hallo—I say, hallo, hallo. [*He puts his face down near its head and calls.*] I say, hallo, Mr. Ugly Face. [*Quick as a wink a pincerlike hand comes out and grabs Tom by his nose. Loudly.*] Yah. Ah—let me go! Yah—ah—you hurt me—let me go!

CREATURE: Then let me go. I want to be quiet. I want to split.

TOM: I won't do a thing, I promise. [*He is released.*] Why do you want to split?

CREATURE: Because my brothers and sisters have all split and turned into beautiful creatures with wings: and I want to split, too. Don't speak to me. I am sure I shall split. I will split. [*It swells and puffs, and creak, puff, bang! it splits all down its back, and out comes a beautiful slim dragonfly. It begins to walk slowly up a slanting stalk.*]

TOM [*in amazement*]: Oh, oh, oh—you beautiful creature, come back. [*He puts up his hand to catch it.*]

DRAGONFLY: No! You cannot catch me. I am a dragonfly now, the king of all flies; and I shall dance in the sunshine and hawk over the river, and catch gnats, and have a beautiful wife like myself. [*It slowly moves its wings.*]

TOM: Oh! Come back, come back, you beautiful creature. I have no one to play with, and I am so lonely here. If you will come back, I will never try to catch you.

DRAGONFLY: I don't care whether you do or not, for you can't. But when I have had my dinner and looked about the world a bit, I'll come back and have a chat with you. Good-by.
[*He climbs to the top and flies away.*]

TOM [*sits sadly down on a stone*]: I am lonely. I'd like to find a water baby like myself to play with.

INSECT [*much smaller than Tom, flies down upon his knee*]: Much obliged to you indeed.

TOM: Obliged for what?

INSECT: For your leg which you are kind enough to hold out for me to sit on. I am a family man—and a very troublesome business it is. So you live under the water?

TOM: Yes, don't you?

INSECT: It's a low place. I have lived here for some time—and very shabby and dirty it is. But I don't choose that it shall last. I shall turn respectable and go to the top.

TOM: I think it is pretty here, only I get lonely, for there are no other water babies.

INSECT: I'm tired of it, that's the truth. I have been quiet and neat and respectable because I'm a family man. Indeed, I've done quite enough business, I consider, to last me my life. Now I shall put on a ball dress and go out and see the gay world.

TOM: And what will become of your wife?

INSECT: Oh, she is a very plain, stupid creature, and that's the truth, and thinks about nothing but eggs. If she chooses to come, why, she may, and if not, why, I go without her—and here I go.

TOM: Why, you're ill! Why, you're dead!

INSECT [*in a high squeaky voice*]: No, I'm not! This is me up here in my ball dress, and that's my skin. Ha-ha! You could not do such a trick as that. Ha-ha! I'm a pretty fellow now, I am. [*His new body is white, his tail orange, his eyes blue, and the whiskers at the end of his tail are five times as long as they were before.*] Oh! Now I shall see the gay world. [*He begins to make his way upward, singing as he goes.*]

My wife shall dance, and I shall sing,
So merrily pass the day.
For I hold it quite the wisest thing
To drive dull care away.

TOM: That was a trick. I wonder if I could do it. I'd like to have wings. I wonder how you begin. What's that? [*A soft sound of half singing, half talking.*]

VOICE: Over I go, and under I go.
I turn, I twist, I dive,
Over I go, and under I go.
It's good to be alive.

[*A lithe, graceful, beautiful, savage otter comes twisting and turning and swimming in. She sees Tom and makes a dash for him.*]

OTTER: Quick, here's something to eat.

[*Tom dodges behind a rock. He can peep out between two rocks safely.*]

OTTER: Come out, or it will be worse for you.

TOM: I won't, I won't. Go away.

OTTER: Then don't. You are not worth eating after all. You are only a nasty eft.

TOM: I am not an eft. Efts have tails.

OTTER: You are an eft. I see your two hands quite plainly, and I know you have a tail.

TOM: I tell you I have not. I ought to know.

OTTER: I say you are an eft, and therefore you are not worth eating by gentlefolks like me. You may stay here until the salmon come, and they will eat you, and we shall eat them. Ha-ha!

TOM: What are salmon?

OTTER: Fish, Eft, great fish, nice fish to eat. They are lords of the fish, and we are lords of the salmon. We hunt them up and down the pools, like this [*she darts about, pretending to hunt*] and drive them up into a corner. They are so proud, until they see us coming, and then they are so meek all at once. We eat them. Their juice is so good, oh, so good. They are coming soon, coming soon. I can smell the rain coming up off the sea, and then hurrah for a fresh salmon, and plenty of eating all day long. [*A low peal of thunder, then a louder one.*]

TOM: Where do they come from?

OTTER: Out of the sea, Eft, the great, wide sea. Out of the sea the salmon come, into the great river down below, and we come up to watch for them. [*Another low peal of thunder and flash of lightning.*] The rain is coming. I can hear it. Away to the sea I must go. [*More thunder and lightning, and darkness grows.*] Now is your time, Eft, if you want to see the world. Down to the sea, down to the sea.

[*She goes out left.*]

TOM: What a jolly thunderstorm.

[*Now the storm comes in earnest, and between flashes of lightning and crashes of thunder are heard many voices calling.*]

VOICES: Down to the sea, down to the sea. [*Trout swim by.*]

TOM: Oh, stay. Wait for me.

VOICES: Down to the sea, down to the sea.

TOM: Down to the sea? Is everything going down to the sea? I will go too.

VOICES [*far and near, soft and loud*]: Down to the sea —down to the sea.

TOM [*joins them*]: Down to the sea, down to the sea.

[*Flashes of lightning and thunder and the sound of rain.*]

## ACT III

[*Under the sea. The backdrop gives the appearance of sand stretching away, with a starfish, sea urchins and seaweed strewn about. There are several rocks at right and left almost covered by seaweed. There are some large rocks on the stage, a lobster trap, and seaweed, shells and curious little sea creatures. It is early dawn, and Tom enters left, calling joyously.*]

TOM: The sea—the sea at last. [*He climbs up on a rock and sits looking toward the stretch of sandy sea floor.*] What a beautiful place this is! I wonder if all the salmon went up the river, and if all the river folks came down to the sea last night? [*A large salmon, shining silver from head to tail, with here and there a dot of crimson, comes swimming by. He stops by the rock on which Tom is sitting.*]

SALMON [*on seeing Tom, asks fiercely*]: What do you want here?

TOM: Oh, don't hurt me! I only want to look at you; you are so handsome.

SALMON: Oh! I really beg your pardon. I see what you are, my little dear. I have met one or two creatures like you before, and found them very agreeable and well behaved. Indeed, one of them showed me a great kindness lately, which I hope to be able to repay.

TOM: So you have seen things like me?

SALMON: Several times, my dear. Indeed, it was only last night that one at the river's mouth came and warned me and my wife of some new nets which had got into the stream since last winter, and showed us the way around them.

TOM: So there are babies in the sea? Then I shall have someone to play with.

SALMON: Were there no babies in the river?

TOM: No! And I grew so lonely. I thought I saw three last night. I have had nothing to play with but caddises and dragonflies and trout.

SALMON: Ugh. What low company. How sad it must have been to live among such people as caddises, silly creatures, and they have six legs, and dragonflies, and as for trout, everyone knows what they are.

TOM: Why do you dislike the trout so?

SALMON: My dear, we do not even mention them if we can help it: for I am sorry to say they are relations of ours who do us no credit. A great many years ago they were just like us, but they were so lazy and cowardly and greedy that instead of going down to the sea every year to see the world they chose to stay and poke about in the little streams and eat worms and grubs.

TOM: And is that why they lost their shining silver coats?

SALMON: That is the reason why they are now brown and spotted and small and ugly.

TOM: Oh, sir, there is a big fierce otter waiting for you and your friends in the river.

SALMON: Thank you for your warning, my dear. Good luck and good-by.

TOM: Oh, what fun, water babies in the sea. But where are they? Oh, here come some strange creatures. What are your names?

[*Purple sea snails floating along, each on a sponge full of foam, five of them.*]

SEA SNAILS: We are called sea snails.

TOM: Where do you come from, you pretty creatures? And have you seen water babies?

SEA SNAILS: Whence we come we know not; and whither we are going, who can tell? We float our lives out in mid-ocean, with the warm sunshine above and the warm Gulf Stream below. Yes, we have seen water babies as we floated along.

[*They float out.*]

TOM: Oh—oh—oh.

[*A large sunfish comes in from behind the large rock.*]

TOM: Oh, who are you?

SUNFISH: I am a sunfish.

TOM: And where are you going?

SUNFISH: I'm sure I don't know. I've lost my way. I meant to go to the Chesapeake, and I'm afraid I've got wrong somehow. Dear me, it is too bad. I'm sure I'm lost.

TOM: Will you play a bit with me?

SUNFISH: Play? I tell you I've lost my way.

TOM: I'm so lonely. Will you let me ride on your back?

SUNFISH: Don't talk to me. I want to think. I've lost my way.
[*Goes out.*]

TOM [*gets down from rock and walks about*]: I must look everywhere; they must be somewhere around.
[*A large lobster comes on, right.*]

LOBSTER: Well, well, well—what are you up to now? Helping some poor fish, I suspect, eh what?

TOM [*turning*]: Oh my! [*He begins to run.*]

LOBSTER: Here, come back, I don't hurt water babies. Although you are meddlesome little creatures without even a shell on your backs.
[*Tom comes back.*]

TOM [*timidly*]: Who—are—you?

LOBSTER: What, don't you know who I am? I'm a lobster—a lobster.

TOM: Oh—and why don't you like water babies?

LOBSTER: I don't dislike them, but they are soft little creatures, always trying to help someone, and they have not even a shell on their backs. I'd be ashamed to be helped by one of them.

TOM: I wish I could find one.

LOBSTER: Oh, you're sure to do so. They are all about.

TOM: I've looked and I've looked.
[*He goes about looking behind rocks and seaweed. The lobster walks into the lobster trap. He tries to get out, but he can't. Tom comes across the screen.*]

LOBSTER: My claws and my pincers, what have I done? It's a trap—a trap—and I cannot get out.

TOM [*spying the lobster*]: Why are you in that thing? Is it your house?

LOBSTER [*with great depression*]: No. I can't get out.

TOM: Why did you get in?

LOBSTER: After that nasty piece of dead fish.

TOM: Where did you get in?

LOBSTER: Through that old hole.

TOM: Then why don't you get out through it?

LOBSTER: Because I can't. I have jumped upwards, downwards, backwards, sideways at least four thousand times; and I can't get out. I can't find the hole.

TOM: Stop a bit. Turn your tail up to me, and I'll pull you through, hind foremost, and then you won't stick on the spikes.

LOBSTER: Are you sure?

TOM: Come along now.

LOBSTER: Are you sure you can?

TOM: Come along, you stupid old stick-in-the-mud, or the fishermen will catch you!

LOBSTER: All right—ready.

TOM: One, two, three, pull. [*Out comes the lobster so fast that Tom falls flat with the lobster on top of him.*]

LOBSTER [*getting up and looking at Tom*]: And a water baby pulled me out—a soft little water baby, without even a shell on its back.

[*A water baby comes in right, sees Tom and runs to him.*]

WATER BABY: Why, you are not one of us, you are a new baby. How wonderful. [*They hug each other and dance around.*]

TOM: Oh, where have you been all this while? I have been looking for you so long, and I have been so lonely.

WATER BABY: We have been here for days and days. There are hundreds of us about the rocks. How was it you did not see us?

TOM: I don't know.

WATER BABY: We romp and sing every evening before we go home.

TOM: I have seen things just like you again and again, but I thought you were shells or sea creatures. It is wonderful!

WATER BABY: Now come and help me, or I shall not have

finished before my brothers and sisters come, and it is time to go home.

TOM: What shall I help you at?

WATER BABY: At this poor dear little rock. A great clumsy boulder came rolling down and rubbed off all its flowers. Now you shall help me make the prettiest little rock garden on all the shore.

[*Enter another water baby.*]

SECOND BABY: Oh, a new water baby—a new water baby.

[*Tom and the second baby hug and dance.*]

FIRST BABY: It's time for Mrs. Doasyouwouldbedoneby to come.

TOM: What a funny long name. Who is she?

FIRST BABY: Don't you know Mrs. Doasyouwouldbedoneby?

TOM: No, indeed.

SECOND BABY: Don't you know her sister, Mrs. Bedonebyasyoudid?

TOM: No, I don't know her either.

FIRST BABY: If you don't know Mrs. Doasyouwouldbedoneby, why did you pull the lobster out of the trap?

TOM: Why, I don't know. But I could not leave him there.

SECOND BABY: Now I know why you have never found us before—I know, I know [*dancing about*].

TOM: Why couldn't I find you? I looked everywhere.

FIRST BABY: Your eyes were shut.

TOM: Oh no, they were not—they were wide open. I could see just everything.

SECOND BABY: But you couldn't see us. You said so.

TOM: Were you really here all the time?

FIRST BABY: Yes, all the time.

SECOND BABY: Here comes Mrs. Doasyouwouldbedoneby. Ask her.

[*Mrs. Doasyouwouldbedoneby enters left and sits down on a seaweed-covered rock. She is the sweetest, kindest, gentlest, most beautiful person one could imagine.*]

MRS. DOASYOUWOULDBEDONEBY: And who are you, you little darling? [*Tom stands apart. The two water babies run to her and lean against her knees.*]

FIRST BABY: He is a new baby—and he has never had a mother.

MRS. DOASYOUWOULDBEDONEBY: Come here, my little one. [*Tom comes and stands by her knee.*]

SECOND BABY: He looked for us ever so long, but he couldn't find us.

MRS. DOASYOUWOULDBEDONEBY: That is because your eyes were shut, my little man.

TOM: I don't understand you, ma'am. I could see the lobster and all the other sea creatures.

MRS. DOASYOUWOULDBEDONEBY: How many sea creatures have you helped?

TOM: Only the lobster.

MRS. DOASYOUWOULDBEDONEBY: Thoughtfulness and kindness open our eyes to many beautiful things in this world.

TOM: Did pulling the lobster out of the trap help me to see the water babies?

WATER BABIES [*dancing around*]: Yes, yes, yes, that is what did it.

TOM: Now I see.

MRS. DOASYOUWOULDBEDONEBY: Of course you do, my dear, and now you are ready to meet my sister, Mrs. Bedonebyasyoudid. Here she comes. Good-by, my dears.

[*Leaves left. Mrs. Bedonebyasyoudid comes in right. She is a stern old lady. She wears a black bonnet and shawl and a pair of large green spectacles on a great hooked nose, hooked so much that the bridge of it is quite above her eyebrows, and under her arm she carries a great birch rod. Tom and two water babies stand in a row before her.*]

MRS. BEDONEBYASYOUDID: So you pulled the lobster out of the trap?

TOM [*timidly*]: Who told you, ma'am?

MRS. BEDONEBYASYOUDID: You did yourself, this very minute.

TOM: But—but——

MRS. BEDONEBYASYOUDID: Yes: everyone tells me exactly what they have done, good or bad, without knowing it themselves. So there is no use trying to hide anything from me.

TOM: That must be hard on people sometimes.

MRS. BEDONEBYASYOUDID [*sternly*]: When they do wrong, it is. However, I am the best friend they ever had. I cannot help punishing people when they do wrong, for I work by machinery just like an engine, and am full of wheels and springs inside, and am wound up very carefully so that I can't help going.

TOM: Was it long ago since they wound you up?

MRS. BEDONEBYASYOUDID: I was wound up once and for all, so long ago I can't remember it. You thought me very ugly just now.

[*Tom hangs his head.*]

I am ugly. I am the ugliest fairy in the world, and I shall be till people behave themselves as they ought to do. Then I shall grow as beautiful as my sister, Mrs. Doasyouwouldbedoneby, who is the most beautiful fairy in the world. Now run away, children, to your play, and leave Tom with me.

[*Water babies go out left.*]

TOM: Tom! Is my name Tom?

MRS. BEDONEBYASYOUDID: Look into my eyes, Tom. Now do you remember?

TOM: Why, I was Tom, the chimney sweep!

MRS. BEDONEBYASYOUDID: So you were, my dear.

TOM: Pray, ma'am, may I ask you a question?

MRS. BEDONEBYASYOUDID: Certainly you may.

TOM: Are the master sweeps, like my master Grimes, punished?

MRS. BEDONEBYASYOUDID: They are, they are indeed, because they knew they were doing wrong. Very severely punished. If the world is to be a happy place, people must learn to like doing right, and to help those they don't like.

TOM: I liked helping the lobster.

MRS. BEDONEBYASYOUDID: But would you like to help your old master Grimes?

TOM: No ma'am, I wouldn't like that. If I should ever find him, he would turn me into a chimney sweep again.

MRS. BEDONEBYASYOUDID: No, he can't do that—no one can ever turn you into a chimney sweep again. Now there are many fine things in the world to see and many things to learn, and the time has come for you to begin your journey.

TOM: Will Master Grimes be at the end of it?

MRS. BEDONEBYASYOUDID: My little man, it is going to take you a long time to find Mr. Grimes, and when you do find him, that will be the beginning.

TOM: Of what?

MRS. BEDONEBYASYOUDID: That is for you to find out.

TOM: Must I go alone?

MRS. BEDONEBYASYOUDID: Always, always.

TOM: I shall be very lonely.

MRS. BEDONEBYASYOUDID: Not at all. If you are brave and honest and good, you will find the world a very interesting and happy place.

TOM: And when I find Master Grimes?

MRS. BEDONEBYASYOUDID: I shall be there when you do. Now you must remember not to be afraid of anything you meet.

TOM: May I say good-by to the water baby I met first?

MRS. BEDONEBYASYOUDID: Here she is.

[*Ellie comes in.*]

Tom is going on a long journey, Ellie.

ELLIE: Dear me! Why, I know you now. You are the very

same little chimney sweep who came into my bedroom.

TOM: Dear me! And I know you, too, now. You are the very same little white lady whom I saw in bed. And now I am going away.

ELLIE: Oh, Tom, what a wonderful adventure. I know you will be brave.

TOM: I am going if it is to the world's end.

MRS. BEDONEBYASYOUDID: And that is a brave, good boy. But you must go farther than the world's end to find Mr. Grimes—for he is at the Other End of Nowhere.

TOM: Then it will be a long journey, so I had better start at once. Good-by, Ellie. I must go out and see the world.

ELLIE: I know you must. But you will not forget me, Tom. I shall wait here till you come.

TOM: I shall not forget you. Good-by, Mrs. Bedonebyasyoudid.

MRS. BEDONEBYASYOUDID: A safe journey to you, Tom.

TOM: Good-by.

## ACT IV

[*The Other End of Nowhere. A large, dull red stone building occupies the center and right of the stage: it is a strange nightmare of a place, with its steeples and towers and battlements and stairways and numerous chimneys large and small. A flight of stairs leads from the left of screen up to a terrace which fairly bristles with chimneys. Mr. Grimes is stuck fast in the largest one, just his head and shoulders showing. He has a battered high black hat on his head, a blue woolen scarf round his neck and an old cob pipe in his mouth. The terrace wall crosses the screen from right to the stairway at the left. On the backdrop is painted a pale yellow sky, deepening to orange, as seen at left of stairway, as it approaches a stretch of blue sea. There is an iron door at the foot of the stairs, and under the wall near right stands a policeman's truncheon. Tom, now a young lad, is stopped by the truncheon as he enters, right.*]

TRUNCHEON: Stop! Your pass!

TOM: It is Mother Carey's pass [*holding up his hand*].

TRUNCHEON: All right—pass on. I had better go with you, young man. [*It hops along beside Tom.*]

TOM: Why have you no policeman to carry you?

TRUNCHEON: Because we are not like those clumsy man-truncheons in the land-world, which need a whole man to carry them about. We do our work ourselves; and do it very well, though I say it who should not.

TOM: Then why have you a thong to your handle?

TRUNCHEON: To hang ourselves up by, of course. When we are off duty.

[*At iron door the Truncheon knocks twice with its own head, the door slides open, Old Brass Blunderbuss appears*].

OLD BRASS BLUNDERBUSS [*in a deep, bell-like voice*]: What case is this?

TRUNCHEON: If you please, sir, it is no case; only a young gentleman from her ladyship, who wants to see Grimes, the master sweep

BLUNDERBUSS: Grimes? Grimes is up chimney No. 345, so the young gentleman had better go on to the roof.

TRUNCHEON: Very good, come along [*as they ascend*], but it's of no use. He is the most unremorseful, hardhearted, foul-mouthed fellow I have in charge, and thinks about nothing but beer and pipes, which are not allowed here, of course. [*They approach Mr. Grimes.*] Attention, Mr. Grimes, here is a gentleman come to see you.

GRIMES: My pipe won't draw, my pipe won't draw.

TRUNCHEON: Keep a civil tongue and attend! [*It pops up and hits Grimes a crack over the head with itself.*]

GRIMES: Hey, stop! Hey! Why, it's Tom! I suppose you have come to laugh at me, ye spiteful little atomy.

TOM: Indeed I have not. I only want to help you.

GRIMES: I don't want anything except beer, and that I can't get; and a light for this bothering pipe, and that I can't get either.

TOM: I'll get you one.

TRUNCHEON: It's no use [*leaning against the chimney and looking on*]. I tell you, it is no use. His heart is so cold that it freezes everything that comes near him. You will see that presently.

GRIMES: Oh, of course it's my fault. Everything's always my fault. Now don't go to hit me again. Ye know if my arms were only free—ye daren't hit me then.

TOM: But can't I help you in any other way? Can't I help you get out of the chimney?

TRUNCHEON: No, he has come to the place where everybody must help himself, and he will find it out, I hope, before he has done with me.

GRIMES: Oh yes, of course it's me. Did I ask to be brought here into this prison? Did I ask to be set to sweep your foul chimneys? Did I ask to stick fast in the very first chimney of all? Did I ask to stay here I don't know how long—a hundred years, I do believe —and never get my pipe, nor my beer, nor anything fit for a beast, let alone a man?

[*Mrs. Bedonebyasyoudid has come in from the right.*]

MRS. BEDONEBYASYOUDID: No, no more did Tom when you behaved to him in the same way.

[*The Truncheon stands upright. Tom makes a low bow.*]

TOM: Oh, ma'am, don't think of me. That's all past and gone, and good times and bad times and all times

"Tom, the Water Baby"
ACT II
Below the river bank

ACT III
Under the sea

ACT IV
The Other End of Nowhere

In the classroom during the making of the cut-out shadow play, "The Carnival of the Animals"

The screen for "The Carnival of the Animals" was forty-two feet long—fastened to wood rollers

pass over. But may I not help poor Mr. Grimes? Mayn't I try and get some of those bricks away?

MRS. BEDONEBYASYOUDID: You may try.

[*Tom tries, but he cannot move one.*]

TOM: Oh dear! I have come all this way, through all those terrible places, to help you, and now I am of no use after all.

GRIMES: Ye had best leave me alone. Ye are a good-natured, forgiving little chap, and that's the truth, but you'd best be off. The hail's coming soon, and it will beat the eyes out of thy little head.

TOM: What hail?

GRIMES: Why, hail that falls every evening here. It's like so much warm rain until it gets close to me—then it turns to hail and knocks me about like small shot.

MRS. BEDONEASYOUDID: That hail will never come any more. It was your mother's tears which your cold heart froze to hail. She is gone to heaven and weeps no more for her wicked son.

GRIMES: So my old mother's gone. And I never there to speak to her. Ah, a good woman she was, living in her little cottage in Vendale at the foot of Lewthwaite Crag.

TOM: Did she live at the foot of the great crag? Then it was she who gave me a drink of milk when I was sick with being chased. She was that kind, even though I was a sweep.

GRIMES: Ah! Good reason she had to hate the sight of a chimney sweep. I ran away from her and took up with sweeps, and never let her know where I was or sent her a penny to help her—and now it's too late—too late. [*He begins crying and blubbering like a great baby. His pipe falls out of his mouth.*] Oh dear, if I was a little chap again with my mother, how different I would be. But it's too late now. So you go along, ye kind little chap, and don't stand to look at a man crying. I am beat now, and beat I must be. Foul I am, and foul I must remain.

MRS. BEDONEBYASYOUDID: Never too late.

[*The bricks begin to loosen about Grimes, and he gets his arms out and begins to climb out of the chimney. The Truncheon jumps up to hit him, but Mrs. Bedonebyasyoudid puts it aside.*]

Will you obey me if I give you a chance?

GRIMES: As you please, ma'am. Ye are stronger than me, I know full well, and wiser than me, I know full well.

MRS. BEDONEBYASYOUDID: So be it, then. You may come out. Take him away and give him his ticket of leave.

TRUNCHEON: What is he to do, ma'am?

MRS. BEDONEBYASYOUDID: Get him to sweep out the crater of Etna—and see to it that crater is never choked again, for if there should be another earthquake I shall investigate the case very severely. Now, Tom, your work here is done. You may go back to This Side of Somewhere.

TOM: I shall be glad to go, ma'am.

MRS. BEDONEBYASYOUDID: Why so glad, Tom?

TOM: Because Ellie is waiting for me. But which way do I go?

MRS. BEDONEBYASYOUDID: There by way of the sea. Ellie is waiting for you by the sea.

TOM: Thank you, Mrs. Bedonebyasyoudid. You have been very kind to me.

MRS. BEDONEBYASYOUDID: If all the world were as good as you and Ellie, I should be as beautiful as my sister, Mrs. Doasyouwouldbedoneby. Good-by, my dear.

TOM: Good-by, dear Mrs. Bedonebyasyoudid.

# THE CHILDHOOD OF DAVID COPPERFIELD

Dramatized from
Charles Dickens' Novel *David Copperfield*

TIME: Nineteenth century.
PLACE: England.

CHARACTERS: David Copperfield
Peggotty
Mrs. Copperfield
Mr. Peggotty
Mrs. Gummidge
Emily
Ham
Mr. Mell
Mr. Creakle
Mr. Tungay
Tommy Traddles
First School Boy
Second School Boy
Third School Boy
James Steerforth
Betsy Trotwood
Janet
Mr. Dick

ACT I: Parlor in Mrs. Copperfield's house.
ACT II: SCENE 1. Inside Mr. Peggotty's boat-house.
SCENE 2. On the beach.
ACT III: In the school room.
ACT IV: Betsy Trotwood's garden.

## ACT I

*[Parlor in Mrs. Copperfield's home. In the center of the back wall is a fireplace; a long window on either side. Peggotty, a buxom, rosy-cheeked woman, in a homespun dress and white apron, sits knitting in an easy armchair at the left of the fireplace. A small table beside her holds her basket of bright-colored wools. David, a slender, fair-haired boy of about seven years, sits on a low stool at the right of the fireplace with an open book on his knees. A straight-backed chair stands a little to the right of David's stool against the back wall between fireplace and window.]*

DAVID [*looking into the fire*]: Peggotty, isn't it nice to be sitting here by the fire?

PEGGOTTY: And indeed it is, but what about that crorkindill book? Go on reading, Master Davy.

DAVID [*reads*]: "The crocodile is a most unpleasant monster to meet. These savage creatures live along the banks of streams and rivers, and lay their eggs in the sand for the sun to hatch. The natives hunt them with long spears, and sometimes even go into the water after them." [*Looking up to ask*]: What would you do, Peggotty, if you were to meet a crocodile?

PEGGOTTY [*stops knitting and looks up*]: Lawk, Master Davy, what a question!

DAVID: But what would you do, Peggotty? You'd have to do something, now wouldn't you?

PEGGOTTY: That you would—and mighty quick, too, if what the book says about those crorkindills is true.

DAVID: I'd have a big spear, Peggotty, the kind the natives use, and I'd put you behind me, and I'd—I'd thrust the spear down the crocodile's throat.

PEGGOTTY: Bless his heart! I believe he would, too. Your

old Peggotty wouldn't be afraid of a hundred crorkindills if she had her Davy alongside of her.

DAVID: A gentleman always protects a lady, Peggotty. That's what my mother says. And if he helps her crossing streets, why, he just naturally would protect her from crocodiles.

PEGGOTTY: Right you are, my pretty.

DAVID: Say, Peggotty, were you ever married?

PEGGOTTY: Lord, Master Davy, what put marriage in your head?

DAVID: But were you ever married, Peggotty? You are a very handsome woman, aren't you?

PEGGOTTY: Me handsome, Davy? Lawk no, my dear. What put that in your head?

DAVID: I don't know, but what is your opinion about it?

PEGGOTTY: My opinion is that I never was married myself, Master Davy, and that I don't expect to be. That's all I know about the subject.

DAVID: You aren't cross, I suppose, Peggotty, are you?

PEGGOTTY: Come here, Davy. [*Opens her arms and gives David a good squeeze.*]

DAVID: My goodness, Peggotty, you hugged me so hard some buttons popped off the back of your dress. I heard them.

PEGGOTTY: Now let me hear some more about the crorkindills—for I an't heard half enough.

DAVID [*reading*]: "When the natives are pursued by crocodiles, they can baffle the vicious creatures by constantly turning as they run. The crocodile is unable to turn quickly, because——"

PEGGOTTY [*interrupting*]: Master Davy, how should you like to go along with me and spend a fortnight at my brother's at Yarmouth? Wouldn't that be a treat?

DAVID: Is your brother an agreeable man, Peggotty?

PEGGOTTY: Oh, what an agreeable man he is [*holding up her hands*]! Then there is the sea, and the boats, and ships, and the fisherman, and the beach, and Am to play with.

DAVID: Peggotty, is your brother's house very, very close to the sea?

PEGGOTTY: That it is. Right by the sea. It is a house-boat.

DAVID: A house-boat, Peggotty?

PEGGOTTY: A boat it used to be, but it's out of reach of the tide now, and it has a chimney and a door cut in the side, and real windows.

DAVID: Why, Peggotty, it must be a most unusual house.

PEGGOTTY: Lawk, Master Davy, I don't know about that, but it's the only one of its kind thereabout, and it's beautifully clean inside and as neat as possible.

DAVID: And how could we get there, Peggotty?

PEGGOTTY: By Mr. Barkis the carrier's cart. We'd have a basket full of lunch, and we'd start directly after breakfast. Now what do you say?

DAVID: Indeed, and what a treat it would be, but what would Mother say?

PEGGOTTY: Why then, I'll as good as bet a guinea that she'll let us go. I'll ask her if you like as soon as ever she comes home. There now.

DAVID: But what's she to do while we are away? She can't live by herself, you know. [*Pause.*] I say, Peggotty, she can't live by herself.

PEGGOTTY: Oh, bless you. Don't you know? She's going to stay with Mrs. Grayper. Mrs. Grayper's going to have a lot of company.

DAVID: Oh, if that is it, I am quite ready to go.
[*Garden bell rings.*]
Quick, Peggotty, there's the bell. I know it's Mother. Let's ask her now. [*He drops his book and stands up.*]

VOICE OUTSIDE: It has been a delightful evening. Good night, good night.
[*Mrs. Copperfield, a delicate, pretty young woman, comes in. Peggotty gets up. David runs to his mother*

*and draws her to the easy chair by the fire. She has a light scarf over her head, which she throws back over her shoulders. Peggotty sits in the straight-backed chair and goes on knitting.*]

DAVID: Mother, Mother dear, Peggotty has invited me to visit her brother's home. It's a house-boat. I want to go very much.

MRS. COPPERFIELD: And you may go, Davy dear. It's very kind of Peggotty to ask you, I am sure.

DAVID: Yes, very, very kind.

MRS. COPPERFIELD: Peggotty, what is this I hear about Mr. Barkis, the carrier—that "Barkis is willing"?

PEGGOTTY [*laughs heartily and throws her apron over her head*]: Oh, ma'am, ma'am!

MRS. COPPERFIELD [*laughing*]: What are you doing, you stupid creature?

PEGGOTTY [*dropping her apron to say*]: Oh, drat the man! He wants to marry me.

MRS. COPPERFIELD: It would be a very good match for you, wouldn't it?

PEGGOTTY: Oh, I don't know. Don't ask me. I wouldn't have him if he was made of gold. Nor I wouldn't have anyone. [*Covers her face with her apron.*]

MRS. COPPERFIELD: Then why don't you tell him so, you ridiculous creature?

PEGGOTTY [*dropping her apron*]: Tell him so? He has never said a word to me about it. He knows better. If he was to make so bold as to say a word to me, I should slap his face.

MRS. COPPERFIELD [*leaning forward*]: Then, Peggotty dear, you are not going to be married?

PEGGOTTY: Me, ma'am? Lord bless you, no!

MRS. COPPERFIELD [*tenderly*]: Not just yet?

PEGGOTTY: Never!

MRS. COPPERFIELD: Don't leave us, Peggotty. What should I ever do without you?

PEGGOTTY: Me leave you, my precious! Not for all the

world and his wife. Me leave you! I think I see myself. Peggotty go away from you? I should like to catch you at it! I'll stay with you until I am a cross, cranky old woman. And when I'm too deaf, and too lame, and too blind, and too mumbly for want of teeth, to be of any use at all, even to be found fault with, then I shall go to my Davy and ask him to take me in.

DAVID: And, Peggotty, I shall be glad to see you, and I'll make you as welcome as a queen.

PEGGOTTY: Bless your heart! I know you will! [*A pause.*] I sometimes wonder, ma'am, what's become of Davy's great-aunt, Miss Betsy Trotwood?

MRS. COPPERFIELD: Lor', Peggotty, what nonsense you talk!

PEGGOTTY: Well, but I really do wonder, ma'am.

MRS. COPPERFIELD: What can have put such a person in your head?

PEGGOTTY: I don't know how it is, but my head never can pick and choose its people. They come and they go, and they don't come and they don't go, just as they like. But I wonder what's become of her.

DAVID: Have I ever seen my great-aunt Betsy Trotwood, Mother?

MRS. COPPERFIELD: No, my child. She was here the night you were born—and we have never seen her since. She used to live in a cottage by the sea, and no doubt she lives there still.

DAVID: Perhaps someday I'll visit her, Mother?

MRS. COPPERFIELD: Goodness no, child. She doesn't like boys.

DAVID [*with disappointment*]: Oh—h—h!

MRS. COPPERFIELD: Now, Davy dear, it's your bedtime.

PEGGOTTY: Come with me, my pet, and I'll light your candle.

DAVID: Good night, Mother dear.

MRS. COPPERFIELD: Good night, Davy dear.

## ACT II

[SCENE I. *Inside Mr. Peggotty's boat-house. The walls are whitewashed. In the back wall is a fire-place; a kettle is hanging over the fire. On top of a chest of drawers, left, there is standing a tea tray, a Bible, a teapot and several cups and saucers. There is a Dutch clock and on the walls several pictures—"Abraham in red about to sacrifice Isaac in blue, and Daniel in yellow coat in a den of green lions." Over the mantel shelf is a picture of the* Sarah Jane *lugger. An armchair stands by the fire-place, left. A small locker at the right of the fire, a table and chair at the right. A locker at extreme left near front of stage. Mrs. Gummidge, a thin woman past middle age, sitting in armchair, is dressed in black, wearing a white apron and cap and a small shawl around her shoulders. Peggotty bustles in with David, right, Sam following.*]

PEGGOTTY: And here we are at last, Master Davy—all snug and warm, and comfortable as can be.

MR. PEGGOTTY [*coming in*]: Well, well, lass, and here you be, and right natural it seems to see you here.

PEGGOTTY: Dan'l, here's young Master Davy.

MR. PEGGOTTY: Glad to see you, sir. You'll find us rough, but you'll find us ready.

DAVID: I am very happy to be here, sir.

MR. PEGGOTTY: And how's your ma? Did you leave her pretty jolly?

DAVID: Yes sir, as jolly as you could wish, and she sent her compliments.

MR. PEGGOTTY: I'm much obliged to her, I am sure. Well, sir, if you can make out here for a fortnight, 'long wi' her [*nodding at Peggotty*] and Ham and little Emily, we shall be proud of your company. [*Turns to Peggotty.*] Lass, have you got the hot water on?

PEGGOTTY: It's all ready, Dan'l.

MR. PEGGOTTY: You see, Master Davy, it's the only thing that will take the dirt off.

[*Goes out left. Emily enters.*]

PEGGOTTY: Master Davy, here is little Emily. She'll show you all the traps and things—such things as you have never seen before.

DAVID: Where, Peggotty? Today?

[*Emily goes and sits on the small rocker by the fireplace.*]

PEGGOTTY: Tomorrow, Davy, bright and early.

DAVID [*going over to Mrs. Gummidge*]: It's nice and cozy here by the fire.

MRS. GUMMIDGE: Cozy for some, but I'm a lone, lorn creetur, and everything goes contrary with me. [*Puts her apron to her eyes.*]

DAVID: I am sorry you are forlorn.

MRS. GUMMIDGE: It's 'cause—— [*Leans forward and sniffs the air.*] Dan'l, Dan'l, this fire's smoking again. Oh, I'm a lone, lorn creetur, and everything goes contrary with me. [*Sobs.*]

PEGGOTTY: It will soon leave off, and besides, you know it's just as disagreeable to us as it is to you.

MRS. GUMMIDGE: No, it ain't. I feel it more.

HAM: Do you want we should open the door?

MRS. GUMMIDGE: Ham Peggotty! Open the door on this cold night, when I'm all shivers and goose flesh, and the creeps is starting in my back again? Oh, oh—I'm a lone, lorn creetur.

PEGGOTTY: It sure is powerful cold, and everybody must feel it so.

[*Goes out.*]

MRS. GUMMIDGE: I feel it more than other folks.

MR. PEGGOTTY [*coming in*]: Well, mates, how are you? [*To Mrs. Gummidge.*] Cheer up, old Mawther! Don't be down! Cheer up for your own sake, only a little bit, and see if a good deal more doesn't come natural!

MRS. GUMMIDGE: Not to me, Dan'l, nothink's natural to me but to be lone and lorn. [*Sobs.*]

MR. PEGGOTTY: No, no.

MRS. GUMMIDGE: Yes, yes, Dan'l.

MR. PEGGOTTY: Cheer up. What's amiss, dame?

MRS. GUMMIDGE: Nothing. You've come from the Willing Mind, Dan'l?

MR. PEGGOTTY: Why yes, I took a spell at the Willing Mind tonight.

MRS. GUMMIDGE: I'm sorry I should drive you there.

MR. PEGGOTTY [*laughing*]: Drive! I don't want no driving. I only go too ready.

MRS. GUMMIDGE: Very ready [*her apron to her eyes*]. Yes, yes, very ready. I am sorry it should be along of me you're so ready.

MR. PEGGOTTY: Along o' you! It ain't along o' you. Don't you believe a bit on it.

MRS. GUMMIDGE: Yes, yes, it is. I know what I am. I know that I'm a lone, lorn creetur, and not only that everything goes contrary with me—but that I go contrary with everybody. Yes, yes, I feel more than other people do, and I show it more. It's my misfortune.

MR. PEGGOTTY: Cheer up, old gal, don't you believe a bit of it.

MRS. GUMMIDGE: I an't what I could wish myself to be. I am far from it. I know what I am. My troubles have made me contrary. I feel my troubles, and they make me contrary. I wish I didn't feel 'em, but I do. I wish I could be hardened to 'em, but I an't. I make the house uncomfortable. I don't wonder at it. I've made your sister so and Master Davy.

DAVID [*fiercely*]: No, you haven't, Mrs. Gummidge.

MRS. GUMMIDGE: It's far from right that I should do it. It an't a fit return. I had better go to the poor house and die. I am a lone, lorn creetur, and had much better not make myself contrary here. If things must go contrary with me, I'd better go into the house and die—and be a riddance. Boo-hoo-oo. [*With her apron to her eyes she goes out of the room. A pause then.*]

MR. PEGGOTTY [*gently*]: She's been thinking of the old 'un!

DAVID: Mr. Peggotty, did you give your son the name of Ham because you lived in a sort of a ark?

MR. PEGGOTTY: No sir, I never give him no name.

DAVID: Who gave him that name, then?

MR. PEGGOTTY: Why, his father give it to him.

DAVID: His father? I thought you were his father.

MR. PEGGOTTY: No, my brother-in-law Joe is his father.

DAVID: Dead, Mr. Peggotty?

MR. PEGGOTTY: Drown dead.

DAVID: Little Emily—she is your daughter, isn't she?

MR. PEGGOTTY: No sir, my brother-in-law, Tom, was her father.

DAVID: Dead, Mr. Peggotty?

MR. PEGGOTTY: Drown dead.

DAVID: Haven't you any children, Mr. Peggotty?

MR. PEGGOTTY: No, master, I'm a bacheldore.

DAVID: A bachelor. Well, about Mrs. Gummidge?

MR. PEGGOTTY: Oh, she's a lorn creetur whose husband——

DAVID: Drowned, Mr. Peggotty?

MR. PEGGOTTY: Aye sir, drown dead.

[*Peggotty enters.*]

PEGGOTTY: So here you are, Master Davy. What would your blessed ma say if she saw you up this time of night?

DAVID: Oh, Peggotty.

MR. PEGGOTTY: There now, Master Davy, run along.

DAVID: Good night, Mr. Peggotty.

MR. PEGGOTTY: Good night, Davy.

DAVID: Good night, Peggotty.
PEGGOTTY: Good night, my pet.
DAVID: Good night, Emily.
EMILY: Good night, Davy.

## ACT II

[SCENE 2. *On the beach. The backdrop shows the distance (left) and a wide stretch of blue water and sky. Some lobster traps are on the stage, left, and some rocks near center right. Emily and David are sitting on two of the largest ones.*]

EMILY [*singing*]: I saw a ship a-sailing, a-sailing on the sea.
And oh, it was laden with pretty things for thee.
There were comfits in the cabin,
And apples in the hold.
The sails were made of silk,
And the mast was made of gold.

DAVID: That is a very pretty song, Emily.
EMILY: "The Fairy Boat" it is called, and I can't help singing it on a day like this, when the sea is blue and sparkling and the sky is so clear. I would not be afraid to sail far out on a day like this.
DAVID: I suppose you're quite a sailor?
EMILY [*shaking her head*]: No, I'm afraid of the sea.
DAVID: Afraid! I am not.
EMILY: Oh, but it's cruel. I have seen it very cruel to some of our men. I've seen it tear a boat as big as our house all to pieces.
DAVID: I hope it wasn't the boat that——
EMILY: That Father drowned in? No, I never saw that boat.
DAVID: Nor him?
EMILY: Not to remember [*shaking her head*].

DAVID: I don't remember my father either. He died when I was very young, and Mother and Peggotty and I live together.

EMILY: Your father was a gentleman, and your mother a lady. And my father and mother were fisher folks. Uncle Dan is a fisherman, too.

DAVID: Dan is Mr. Peggotty, is he?

EMILY: Uncle Dan yonder [*nodding toward the boat-house*].

DAVID: He must be very good, I should think.

EMILY: Good? If I was ever to be a lady, I would buy him a sky-blue coat with diamond buttons, a cocked hat, nankeen trousers, a red velvet waistcoat, a large gold watch, a silver pipe, and I would give him a box of money.

DAVID: I am sure he deserves all the treasures you have mentioned. You would like to be a lady, Emily?

EMILY: I should like it very much. We would all be gentlefolks together then, me and Uncle and Ham and Mrs. Gummidge. We wouldn't mind it then, when there come stormy weather. Not for our own sakes, I mean. We would for the poor fishermen's, to be sure, and we'd help 'em with money when they come to any hurt. [*Laughing.*] Don't you think you are afraid of the sea now?

DAVID: No, and you don't seem to be, though you say you are.

EMILY [*getting up as she speaks*]: Oh, I'm not afraid of the sea when it is quiet like this, but I wake when the wind blows, and tremble to think of Uncle Dan and Ham, and believe I hear 'em crying out for help. That's why I should like to be a lady so much. But I'm not afraid this way—not a bit. How do you like our house, David?

DAVID: I don't believe there ever was a more interesting house. There are so many things to look at and to ask questions about.

EMILY: I'm glad you like it. It is the only house I remember.

DAVID: And it has such a different smell. Even my pocket handkerchief smells exactly as if it had wrapped up a lobster.

EMILY: Oh, that's because we are fisher folks. Uncle Dan keeps lobsters, crabs and crawfish in those big kegs over yonder. But I never notice the smell of 'em. I'm so used to it.

DAVID: I'd like to stay here forever. That is if my mother could be here, too.

EMILY: Perhaps if you tell her how happy you are here——

DAVID: Peggotty says I have a new father, and that we must go home tomorrow, and that I shall most likely be sent away to school.

EMILY: Oh, Davy, Davy, I'll miss you so.

DAVID: I'll miss you, too, Emily, and think of you every day. You are the most beautiful, beautiful——

HAM [*appearing*]: Hie, mates. What luck in the digging? A pail full of clams, and I'll wager my new boots.

EMILY [*eagerly*]: Oh, Ham, please whistle the horn pipe, and, Davy, you dance.

DAVID: Oh, but I don't know the steps very well, Emily, and some of them get all mixed up.

EMILY: Never mind, Davy, please try. Ham, now whistle.

HAM: All right, my hearties. Now then, Master Davy, here goes.

[*Whistles the "Sailor's Horn Pipe." Davy dances in spirited fashion.*]

EMILY: Oh, that was fine, Davy.

HAM: Right-o, my little mate.

PEGGOTTY [*calling from without*]: Davy, Emily, Ham.

DAVID [*shouting*]: We're coming.

EMILY: We're coming.

## ACT III

[*In the school room. A most forlorn and desolate place. The walls are dirty and splashed with ink. There are three rows of benches and desks, scraps of copy books and exercises litter the desks and floor. A miserable white mouse is confined in a poor-looking cage made of pasteboard and wire. There are two desks and chairs at the left for the masters. On one of these is lying a large placard covered with writing.*]

VOICES OUTSIDE [*gruffly*] : So you're the new boy?

DAVID [*outside*] : Yes sir.

VOICE : Go in the school room and wait.

DAVID : Yes sir. [*Enters and looks around.*] Oh, what a dismal room, what a dingy, dirty old room! What would Peggotty think? [*He sees the large card on the desk.*] What's printed on this placard? [*Reads.*] "Take care of him. He bites." [*David climbs up on the desk.*] There must be a big vicious dog around somewhere; it's safest up here.

[*Mr. Mell enters.*]

MR. MELL. What are you doing up there?

DAVID : I beg your pardon, sir, but I'm afraid of the dog.

MR. MELL : Dog? What dog?

DAVID : Isn't it a dog?

MR. MELL : Isn't what a dog?

DAVID : That's to be taken care of, sir, that bites?

MR. MELL : No, Copperfield, that's not a dog. That's a boy. My instructions are to put this placard on your back. I am sorry to make such a beginning with you, but I must do it.

[*David gets down, and Mr. Mell ties the cardboard onto David's shoulders.*]

MR. MELL : Now tell me, Copperfield, what do you like to bite?

DAVID: Oh, please, sir, I don't like to bite at all, but my stepfather, Mr. Murdstone, was beating me—and——

MR. MELL: Ah, I see. Well, Copperfield, I fear you will have a hard time of it when Mr. Creakle comes in, and the boys. I'm sorry for you.

[*Leaves room. Tommy Traddles enters, with his slate covered with skeletons.*]

TRADDLES: Hello. Who are you?

DAVID: I'm David Copperfield, the new boy. What's your name?

TOMMY: Traddles, Tommy Traddles. Ever been away to school before?

DAVID: Never.

TOMMY: Too bad your family sent you here. Mr. Creakle is a tartar—he'll tell you so himself—and Mr. Tungay, his assistant, is a bully. Mr. Mell isn't bad; he is the man who tied that card on you. Mr. Creakle made him do it. Now I say, Copperfield, don't you feel bad about that card. See here [*holds up his slate*].

DAVID: It's covered with drawings of skeletons.

TOMMY: Yes, when things go badly with me, I draw skeletons—makes me feel better.

DAVID: When the boys come, they will see the placard. They will torment me.

TOMMY: Look here—let's make it a game. Leave it to me. Hello.

[*Several boys come in.*]

How's Traddles?

Who's the new one?

Oh, I say [*looking at card*].

TOMMY: This is my friend Towzer.

FIRST BOY: Shake a paw.

SECOND BOY: Bow-wow.

THIRD BOY: Lie down, sir.

[*They dance and laugh around David. Steerforth enters.*]

STEERFORTH: So you're the new boy. Copperfield's your name?

DAVID: Yes, sir.

[*Boys move away.*]

STEERFORTH: I'm J. Steerforth, the head boy here. I heard the row, and I say, that card you're wearing is a jolly shame. Now I'll do something for you. What money have you got, Copperfield?

DAVID: Seven shillings.

STEERFORTH: You had better give it to me to take care of. At least, you can if you like. You needn't if you don't like.

DAVID: I do like it, and it's very friendly of you.

STEERFORTH: Do you want to spend anything now?

DAVID: No, thank you.

STEERFORTH: You can if you like, you know. Say the word.

DAVID: No, thank you, sir.

STEERFORTH: Perhaps you'd like to spend a couple of shillings or so in a bottle of currant wine by and by, up in my bedroom. You belong to my bedroom, I find.

DAVID: Yes, I should like that.

STEERFORTH: Very good. You'll be glad to spend another shilling or so in almond cakes, I dare say?

DAVID: Yes, I should like that, too.

STEERFORTH: And another shilling or so in biscuits, and another in fruit, eh? I say, young Copperfield, you're going it!

DAVID: Yes, it looks that way, sir.

STEERFORTH: Well, we must make it stretch as far as we can; that's all. I'll do the best in my power for you. I can go out when I like, and I'll smuggle the things in. Don't be uneasy, Copperfield. I'll take care of things.

DAVID: Oh, thank you, thank you very much.

STEERFORTH: And a royal spread we'll have. Say, Copperfield, you're a daisy, a very daisy. The flower of the field at sunrise is not more innocent. You don't mind my calling you Daisy, do you, my young friend?

DAVID: Oh no, not at all.

STEERFORTH: Here, Traddles, look after our young friend here.

TRADDLES: What's the matter? Need cheering up? Shall I draw you some skeletons?

[*Mr. Creakle enters, followed by Mr. Tungay.*]

MR. CREAKLE: So! This is the young gentleman whose teeth are to be filled. Hey! Turn him around.

[*Mr. Tungay brings David forward.*]

Now what's the report of this boy?

TUNGAY: There's nothing against him yet. There has been no opportunity.

[*Boys sit down on benches.*]

MR. CREAKLE: Come here, sir!

MR. TUNGAY: Come here!

MR. CREAKLE: I have the happiness of knowing your stepfather, and a worthy man he is, and a man of strong character. He knows me and I know him. Do you know me? Hey?

DAVID: Not yet, sir.

MR. CREAKLE: Not yet? Hey? But you will soon. Hey?

MR. TUNGAY: You will soon. Hey.

MR. CREAKLE: I'll tell you what I am. I'm a tartar!

MR. TUNGAY: A tartar.

MR. CREAKLE: When I say I'll do a thing, I'll do it. When I say I will have a thing done, I will have it done.

MR. TUNGAY: . . . will have a thing done, will have it done.

MR. CREAKLE: I'm a determined character. That's what I am. I do my duty. That's what I do. Now you have begun to know me, my young friend. You may go. Take him away.

DAVID [*timidly*]: If you please, sir——

MR. CREAKLE: Hah! What's this?

DAVID: If you please, sir, I am very sorry for what I did. If I might be allowed to take this card off——

MR. CREAKLE [*threatening him*]: Hah! Hah!
[*David retreats.*]
Boys, in your seats.

MR. TUNGAY: In your seats.

MR. CREAKLE: Now this is a new half. Take care what you're about in this new half. Come fresh up with the lessons, I advise you, for I come fresh up with the punishments. I won't flinch. It will be of no use your rubbing yourselves. You won't rub the marks out that I give you. Now to work, every boy. That's that. Silence!

TOMMY: How you tremble, Copperfield! You will have to get used to his roar.

MR. CREAKLE: Put your slates down, and study the lessons on the board.

DAVID: Someday I shall run away. I'll go to my aunt Betsy Trotwood.

## ACT IV

[*Betsy Trotwood's garden. A window and low-hanging eave of the house is visible at left. Flowers are in the window; below the window is a garden bench, and at the back of the stage a wall in which there is a gate. There are many flowers and vines growing against the wall, and a few flower pots standing near the house end of the wall. Miss Betsy is a tall, stern-looking woman, rather handsome, though unbending and austere. Her dress is of a lavender color, scantily made. She wears a cap and loose gloves. She is holding a watering can and is bending over the plants when David, travel-worn and ragged,*

Elephants—"The Carnival of the Animals"

Kangaroos

Aquarium—"The Carnival of the Animals"

The long-eared characters

*enters at the gate. He comes in timidly. Miss Betsy does not see him. He comes up to her and touches her shyly. She looks up quickly and exclaims.*]

MISS BETSY: Go away! Go along! No boys here!

DAVID: If you please, ma'am. [*Pause.*] If you please, Aunt.

MISS BETSY [*in amazement*]: Eh!

DAVID: If you please, Aunt, I am your nephew.

MISS BETSY: Oh, Lord! [*Sits down on the garden path.*]

DAVID: I am David Copperfield, of Blunderstone, in Suffolk—where you came on the night when I was born, and saw my dear mother. I have been very unhappy since she died. I have been slighted, and taught nothing, and thrown upon myself and put to work not fit for me. It made me run away to you.

MISS BETSY: Mercy! Mercy!

DAVID: I was robbed at first setting out, and I have walked all the way, and have never been in a bed since I began the journey. [*He sinks down on the garden seat and cries silently. His aunt comes over to him.*]

MISS BETSY: Mercy on us! Mercy on us! [*She calls.*] Janet, Janet.

JANET [*at door*]: Yes, ma'am.

MISS BETSY: Janet, go upstairs with my compliments to Mr. Dick, and say I wish to speak to him. [*A pause.*] Mercy on us. Lie down, child. [*To Mr. Dick*]: Mr. Dick, don't be a fool, because nobody can be more discreet than you can when you choose. We all know that. So don't be a fool, whatever you are.

MR. DICK [*vaguely*]: A fool? Me a fool?

MISS BETSY: Mr. Dick, you have heard me mention David Copperfield? Now don't pretend not to have a memory, because you and I know better.

MR. DICK: David Copperfield? David Copperfield. Oh yes, to be sure. David, certainly.

MISS BETSY: Well, this is his boy, his son. He would be as

like his father as it's possible to be, if he was not so like his mother, too.

MR. DICK: His son? David's son? Indeed?

MISS BETSY: Yes, and he has done a pretty piece of business. He has run away. Now here you see young David Copperfield, and the question I put to you is, what shall I do with him?

MR. DICK [*feebly*]: What shall you do with him? Oh! Do with him?

MISS BETSY: Yes, come! I want some very sound advice.

MR. DICK: Why, if I was you—I should [*briskly*] I should wash him!

MISS BETSY: Janet, Mr. Dick sets us all right. Heat the bath. There, child, now there, there, child. I suppose you think Mr. Dick a short name?

DAVID: Rather a short name, Aunt.

MISS BETSY: You are not to suppose that he hasn't got a longer name, if he chose to use it. Babley, Mr. Richard Babley, that's the gentleman's true name. But don't call him by it, whatever you do. He can't bear his name. That's a peculiarity of his. So take care, child, you don't call him anything but Mr. Dick. Now I'll leave you with Mr. Dick.

MR. DICK: You have been to school, David?

DAVID: Yes sir, for a short time.

MR. DICK: Do you recollect the date when King Charles I had his head cut off?

DAVID: I believe, sir, it happened in the year 1649.

MR. DICK: Well, so the books say: but I don't see how that can be, because if it was so long ago, how could the people about him have made that mistake of putting some of the trouble out of his head into mine?

DAVID: That's very strange, Mr. Dick.

MR. DICK: It is very strange. And I never can get that quite right. I never can make that perfectly clear. But no matter. What do you think of that for a kite?

DAVID: I think it is a beautiful one, and I have never seen one so big.

MR. DICK: I made it. We'll go and fly it, you and I. Do you see this [*pointing to the paper of which the kite is made*]?

DAVID: Why, it's covered with writing.

MR. DICK: Facts—all facts. There's plenty of string, and when it flies, it takes the facts a long way. I don't know where they may come down. It's according to circumstances and so forth; but I take my chance of that. I'll go try it now.

[*Mr. Dick goes out with his kite. Miss Betsy enters.*]

MISS BETSY: Well, child, what do you think of Mr. Dick?

DAVID: Is he—is Mr. Dick at all out of his mind?

MISS BETSY: Not a morsel!

DAVID: Oh, indeed.

MISS BETSY: If there is anything in the world Mr. Dick is not, it's that.

DAVID: Oh, indeed.

MISS BETSY: He is a distant connection of mine. He has been called mad by his family, but he is the most friendly and amenable creature in existence. And as for advice! But nobody knows what that man's mind is but myself. [*Pause.*] Did he say anything to you about King Charles I?

DAVID: Yes, Aunt.

MISS BETSY: Oh! That's his allegorical way of expressing it. He connects his illness with great disturbance and agitation, naturally, and that's the figure he chooses to use. And why shouldn't he, if he thinks it proper?

DAVID: Certainly, Aunt.

MISS BETSY: It's not a business-like way, nor a worldly way. I'm aware of that.

DAVID: Yes, Aunt.

MISS BETSY: And I say again, nobody knows what that man's mind is except myself; and he's the most amenable and friendly creature in existence. If he likes to fly a kite sometimes, what of that?

DAVID: Certainly, Aunt.

MISS BETSY: Franklin used to fly a kite.

DAVID: Yes, Aunt.

MISS BETSY: He was a Quaker or something of that sort if I'm not mistaken. And a Quaker flying a kite is a much more ridiculous object than anybody else.

DAVID: Yes, Aunt.

MISS BETSY: Mr. Dick [*as Mr. Dick enters*], when this child has had a bath and his supper and a good night's sleep—what shall I do with him?

MR. DICK: Why—why have him measured for a suit of clothes.

MISS BETSY: Mr. Dick, give me your hand, for your common sense is invaluable. David, how would you like to live here with Mr. Dick and me?

DAVID: Oh, Aunt, I would like it very much.

MISS BETSY: Mr. Dick, you'll consider yourself guardian jointly with me of this child.

MR. DICK: I shall be delighted to be the guardian of David's son.

MISS BETSY: Very well, that's settled. I have been thinking, do you know, Mr. Dick, I might call him Trotwood.

MR. DICK: Certainly, certainly, call him Trotwood, certainly, David's son, Trotwood.

MISS BETSY: Trotwood Copperfield, you mean?

MR. DICK: To be sure, yes, Trotwood Copperfield.

DAVID: Oh, I am so happy. I have found a home at last.

# PART II

# Shadow Plays with Music

## CHAPTER III

## Selecting the Shadow Play to Be Given with Music

In almost every shadow play, music has some part, perhaps a very small part, such as a whistled tune, dance music for a jig or the singing of a folk song.

Incidental music, when it has been carefully chosen and used appropriately, always adds to the interest and pleasure of the audience. You may not know that there are shadow plays given almost entirely to music, or that there is a wealth of such material for you to use.

Here are a few suggestions. You can use nursery songs, Christmas carols, old ballads, scenes from the operas and music for which there are no words. These last are tone poems that describe to you as clearly as words do, the picture that was in the composer's mind when he wrote down the notes.

Nursery songs would make delightful shadow plays for the entertainment of very young children. "I Saw Three Ships Go Sailing By on Christmas Day in the Morning." How fanciful and charming this would be as a shadow play! The scenery, properties and figures colorful and translucent in the manner of the Chinese shadow play.

"A Frog Who Would A-wooing Go, Whether His Mother Would Let Him or No" would make a merry shadow play.

"On the Bridge of Avignon" would send us to books and pictures to see what kind of a bridge we would need for this old French town. What kind of houses would we paint in the background? According to the words of the song, all the world dances on the bridge. Of course this means the world of Avignon, boys and girls, men and women in peasant costumes. Perhaps the cats and dogs joined in the merrymaking. A happy song to sing and to use for a shadow play.

In the book *Songs from Many Lands,* compiled by Thomas W. Surette, you will find many old friends and make some new ones.

A very beautiful Christmas program could be worked out with carols as the musical background. If one made a shadow play of "As Shepherds Watched Their Flocks by Night," both opaque and translucent figures could be used. The foreground and shepherds in black silhouette; the distant hills and far-away Bethlehem in color; the figures of the angels translucent. If the nearest angels are merely outlined forms, the light would give them a luminous whiteness. The more distant and smaller figures should be less transparent. For directions for making opaque and translucent figures, read Chapter II in the first section.

"Bring a Torch, Jeannette, Isabelle" is a French carol that would make a fine shadow play—sprightly but full of tenderness and feeling.

*The Oxford Book of Carols* is an excellent book for helping you to find carols for a Christmas program.

The cuckoo in the depths of the wood

Aviary—"The Carnival of the Animals"

The pianists and the fossils

The Swan—"The Carnival of the Animals"

And don't overlook "Good King Wenceslaus."

Scenes from well-known operas might be given by a group interested in opera. Members of the group could sing some of the simpler arias—or if that proved too difficult, there are excellent gramophone records to be had.

What would make a more delightful shadow opera than "Hansel and Gretel"?

*Sadko,* the opera composed by Rimsky-Korsakoff, became the theme for a shadow play given by twenty-eight ninth-grade girls and boys. They read the libretto and listened to gramophone records of the opera. They studied Russian architecture and costumes, and were brimful of ideas and enthusiasm when they started work on their play. Sixty brilliantly colored and well-designed figures were made on the principle of the Chinese shadow figures. Scenes were painted on glass and projected onto the screen. There were spoken words as well as a musical accompaniment for the action of the play.

As to shadow plays given to music without a word being spoken or sung, at first this might seem the most simple kind of play to give—no words to memorize, merely the figures to be moved about. However, the success of this kind of play depends upon the action of the figure in response to the music. Perhaps you have seen a ballet, where the dancers moved so harmoniously to the music that it seemed as though the music moved the dancers. That is exactly the feeling that you should give your audience. It requires a good bit of skill and a great deal of practice to manipulate a figure to music.

What could be more delightful and entertaining than to take the musical joke by Camille Saint-Saëns, which he called the "Carnival of the Animals," into the world of shadows? Here are musical notes which suggest the tramp of elephants, the roar of lions, the crowing and cackling of cocks and hens, the slow movements of turtles, the hopping and jumping of kangaroos, notes which are beautiful as well as humorous because there is a finely arranged pattern of tone and melody.

In the tone picture called "Aquarium" there is a graceful, rippling movement suggesting fish among gently swaying water plants. Perhaps you will think the swan is the loveliest tone picture of them all. A great dancer, Anna Pavlowa, gave an exquisite interpretation of this music.

You may think the most amusing picture is that of a certain type of pianist whose fingers dash up and down the scales, every now and then striking a wrong note, who bangs and fumbles and goes on and on, his long-tailed coat and moppy hair flying about. Saint-Saëns enjoyed poking fun at this kind of musician.

If you listen to the music of the "Carnival of the Animals," and then look at the photographs of the play made by a ninth-grade group, you will see how much the pupils were influenced by the music in designing their scenes.

Have you ever heard Debussy's tone poem, "An Afternoon of a Faun"? This strange, fascinating, exotic figure of a faun would be a creature of the forest and stream, resembling the Greek God Pan—pointed ears, horns, a tail and cloven feet. A wild, furtive creature that loves music and the depths of the woods. Try to imagine a faun stretched on a great rock near a stream, playing on his flute and enjoying the golden shafts of afternoon sunlight. Perhaps his music lured the water nymphs from the stream to dance to his music—swiftly, gracefully; perhaps even the hares and little wild things of the woods came to listen to his playing, and then gradually the sunlight paled and the shadows of the evening closed in, and the dreamlike afternoon was ended.

A Greek poet long ago made a picture in woods describing just such a scene as Debussy described in music. He wrote:

*Be still, ye wooded cliffs and water falls*
*And mingled bleatings of the murmuring meads!*
*For Pan with sweetly ringing music calls,*
*Laying his lip on pipe of bounden reeds.*
*And round him dancing swift with glimmering feet*
*Nymphs of the forest and the fountain meet.*

A famous Russian composer, Igor Stravinsky, wrote the music for a brilliant and dramatic ballet called "Petrouchka." You may have heard it played by a symphony orchestra and recall how at one time the instruments make a pattern of notes that suggest a fair or circus. There are so many different sounds that at first all seems confusion. However, if you listen intently, you can pick out groups of notes that make pictures: the merry-go-round, the dancers, the hawkers crying their wares, even the big lumbering bear and his whistling master, the organ-grinder, and of course Petrouchka, the ballerina and the Moor, dancing madly in their little booth while the showman plays on his small flute.

How colorful it is, and what could be more fun than to make all these brightly flashing pictures come to life on a shadow screen.

There is tragedy in this ballet as well as merriment and fun. There is laughter and tears, joy and sorrow. The shadow screen is a mirror of life itself, a mingling of light and shade. And so little Petrouchka falls in love with the dainty ballerina who dances light-heartedly through all the scenes, and the Moor loves the ballerina, too, and through jealousy and rage kills Petrouchka, but Petrouchka's spirit leaps away unharmed ready for new adventure.

Have you ever listened to Stravinsky's beautiful music for the "Fire Bird"? Magical music that suggests numerous pictures and figures for a glowing, colorful shadow play.

Claude Debussy, who composed "An Afternoon of a Faun," also wrote a suite for the piano called "The Children's Corner," which has delightful possibilities for a shadow play. Think of designing scenery and figures for:

The Golliwogg's Cake Walk
The Snow Is Falling
The Serenade for the Doll
The Shepherd

We are very fortunate today in having so much beautiful music, played by our finest symphony orchestras and musicians, recorded and ready for our use.

Gramophone records are not expensive, and if your local music stores do not have the particular record you wish, they will be glad to order it for you. However, there are many shadow plays in which music plays only an incidental part. For plays of this kind you should choose appropriate music and the right musical instruments.

Have you ever tried to make a musical instrument? If you have not, you will be surprised to hear that there are many different kinds of instruments that you can make from the materials that you see and use every day; materials and objects which you do not associate with musical tone, pitch or melody.

Wooden chopping bowls, hollow cocoanut shells, gourds and butter tubs, covered with sheepskin or heavy paper, make excellent drums. Each drum will have its own particular tone.

What is the tone of a drinking glass? Strike one lightly with a pencil or stick and listen for the clear, bell-like sound. Put a little water in the glass, and the tone will be changed. If you put different quantities of water into several glasses, you will discover that by regulating the amount of water in the glasses you can tune them to a tone scale, and by striking the side of the glass play a melody upon them.

Hunting for tone quality in different objects is a fascinating game—pieces of wood, metal, bottles, jugs, china and hollow reeds have surprising possibilities.

The tone quality of a piece of wood depends upon its length and thickness. A scale could be developed by graduating the lengths. A wooden instrument of the marimba type can be made. Then there are stringed instruments of many kinds—lyres, banjos, fiddles—constructed from hollow cocoanut shells or cigar boxes. The shepherd's pipe and Pan-pipes can be made from hollow reeds. Have you ever blown directly across the open end of a reed?

The following musical instruments can be made by boys and girls: drums, rattles, tambourines, trumpets, Pan-pipes, shepherds' pipes, oboes, flutes, harps, lyres, lutes, fiddles and banjos. There is a great deal of joy in experimenting in a new field. Why not make your own instrument for your play? A circus clown or a dancing bear capers to a tune played on a drum or a pipe of your own making; a dainty lady dances to a lute or sings to the accompaniment of a lyre; an Indian medicine man performs to the measured beat of a tom-tom or the staccato sound of a rattle.

The rightness of your choice of a musical instrument for the incidental music of your play does a great deal in adding to the beauty of it.

In *Creative Music for Children,* by Satis N. Coleman, published by G. P. Putnam's Sons, you will find many suggestions for making your own musical instruments.

# CHAPTER IV

## The Carnival of the Animals

### A CUT-OUT SHADOW PLAY PERFORMED TO MUSIC

WHEN Camille Saint-Saëns composed the "Carnival of the Animals," he could scarcely have imagined that many years later it would inspire a delightful and humorous shadow play. The experiences that a group of ninth-year junior high school pupils had in making their "shadows" may prove helpful to you in making your shadow plays.

This group of twenty-two girls and boys elected an art course which gave them two consecutive periods of art every day. They were not especially talented, but they all liked to draw, paint and to make things.

When Miss Lillian Baldwin, supervisor of music appreciation in the Cleveland Public Schools, heard that this group wished to give a shadow play, she suggested the "Carnival of the Animals," and came to their art room with victrola records of this musical suite. She told them something about the very interesting composer, Saint-Saëns, and how he came to write this piece of music, so different from the music we usually hear.

In the Old World there is a very gay carnival time that comes before the season of Lent. In our own country the city of New Orleans in Louisiana has celebrated Mardi Gras for many years. You may have seen pictures in the movies of the spectacular floats and the crowds of merrymakers in costumes and masks, dancing and singing in the streets. Music and laughter everywhere! Lent is a quiet, thoughtful season, and into this last day before Lent the people crowd the hours with frolic and fun.

Saint-Saëns wrote the "Carnival of the Animals" for one of the Carnival Concerts in Paris. It is very humorous, also beautiful. A delicious musical joke! If you listen, you will recognize all the different animals that Saint-Saëns is describing.

The royal march of the lions! What dignity, how pompous he is, this king of the beasts. Hear him growl, and what a mighty roar!

How amusing to see hens and cocks follow so grand a creature. Here they are pecking and clucking; the cock gives a strident cock-a-doodle-do.

Can you imagine a tune slow enough for turtles? Saint-Saëns took a very fast time from a popular opera and made it into a slow, dragging tune for the turtles. A good musical joke. The carnival goes on—elephants, kangaroos, fish, long-eared persons that kick and he-haw—and then comes an exquisite tone picture, the cuckoo in the depths of the woods. The music describes the deep, cool woods, the stillness and the call of the cuckoo, now far, now near.

Would you ever expect to find pianists in a carnival of animals? How very funny these creatures are. Saint-Saëns took great pleasure in satirizing a certain type of musician. Before the pianists leave the scene, the fossils come in to give a jerky dance. Last comes

*Finale*—"The Carnival of the Animals"

A long-eared character and a turtle as they looked behind the scenes in "The Carnival of the Animals"

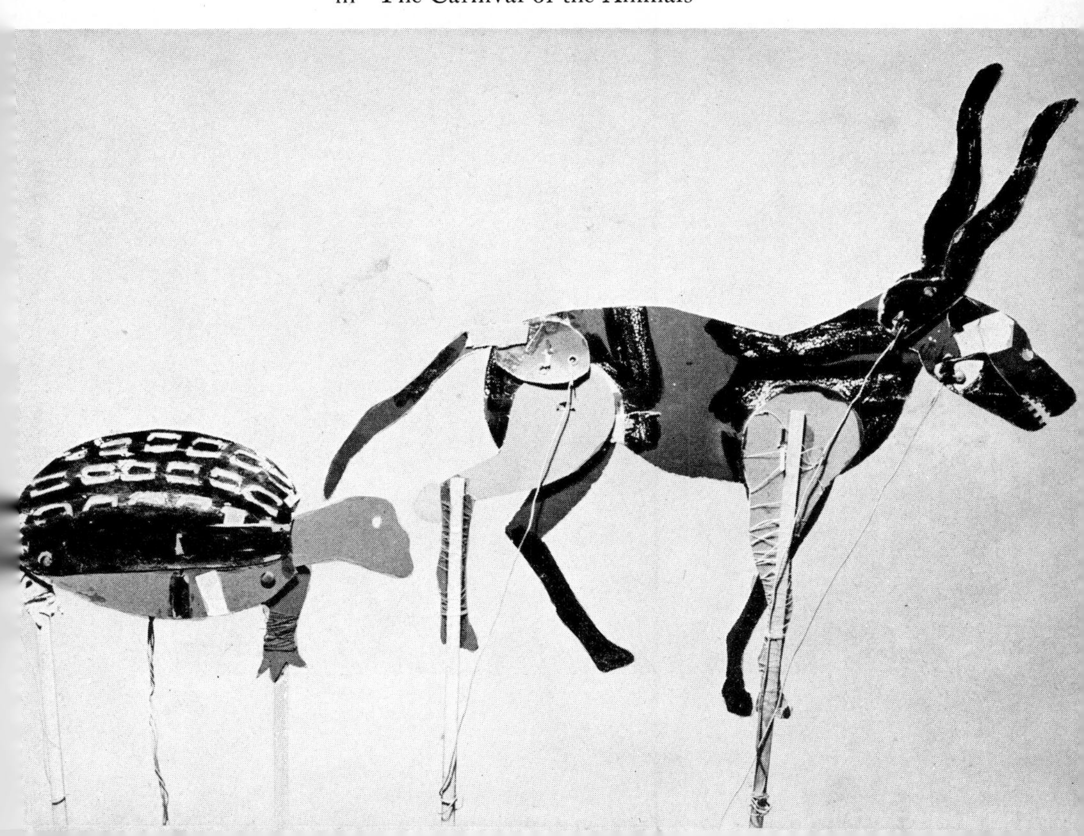

Behind the screen at the Cleveland Museum of Art during a performance of the human shadow play, "The Indian and the Oki"

"The Indian and the Oki"

the lovely swan, a tone picture that sets one to dreaming of an enchanted lake, bending willows and floating clouds. When the dream is over, back come all the animals for the finale, all but the stately swan.

"The Carnival of the Animals" is ended, but the tunes keep singing in one's head.

"The Carnival of the Animals" is described by Miss Baldwin in her study material for the Children's Concerts given by the Cleveland Symphony Orchestra. The material is published by A. S. Gilman, Cleveland, Ohio.

After hearing the Carnival Suite there was a discussion period for the purpose of planning the play. The first question was, what kind of a screen would be most satisfactory? The music allowed no time for changing scenes, and a wait between the numbers would spoil the musical effect.

One of the pupils suggested using a long strip of material on which all the scenes could be painted, one after another. This idea was well received.

A list of the scenes was then made. The first six musical numbers could be given without a change of scene.

SCENE I—March of the Lions
Hens and Cocks
Fleet-footed Animals
Turtles
Elephants
Kangaroos
SCENE II—Aquarium
SCENE III—Long-eared Persons

SCENE IV—Cuckoo in the Depths of the Wood
SCENE V—Aviary
SCENE VI—Pianists
Fossils
SCENE VII—The Swan
SCENE VIII—Finale

A wood frame with an opening three by five feet was needed, also two vertical rollers with ratchets and handles.

Five feet was allowed for each scene, an extra two feet in case of need. A strip of fine nainsook forty-two feet long was purchased. This was wet and stretched along one side of the room and then brushed lightly with a sizing. When the material dried, the sizing prevented the color, used in painting, from spreading. The sizing was made as follows: ten or fifteen cents worth of gum arabic in about one quart of water. After the gum arabic is dissolved (this takes several hours), brush lightly over the wet screen. Either a large brush or a piece of cloth can be used for brushing the sizing over the wet surface. Later gypsy dyes were used in painting the material. They are brilliant in color and easy to handle.

After the question of the screen had been answered, the next question was how to design the scenes. Each student designed one or more scenes, using crayons on large sheets of unprinted newspaper. The sketches were discussed, the best points in each commented upon and a committee of eight students chosen to be responsible for the designing and painting of the scenes. The photographs show the group at work in the art room. Some at work on the screen, others upon the shadow figures.

The problem of making the figures raised the question of their size. Some were close to fourteen inches tall. From the photographs you will see the relation of the size of the figure to the screen.

The figures used in the fourth scene, "The Cuckoo in the Depths of the Wood," were small to emphasize the feeling of deep space and solitude. There was very little action in this scene, just the lifting of the deer's head when the cuckoo calls, the slow, graceful movements of the doe, and the little fleet-footed rabbits.

Many excellent pictures of animals were borrowed from the library and studied carefully before the drawings were made. Stiff cardboard was used for all the figures. The parts were traced onto the cardboard and cut out with a razor blade. The figures of the long-eared figure and the turtle in the photograph had been used many times and undergone a good deal of repair by the time the picture was made. The thread around the legs was used to reinforce the glued sticks.

The wings of the swans, the backs of the turtles and the bodies of the fish were enriched by pattern. The designs were cut out with a sharp knife or razor blade. The turtles were so constructed that their necks and heads could be pulled back under the shell. The trunks of the elephants were constructed according to the drawing. They moved naturally.

There were between fifty and sixty shadow figures made for this one play. The large animals were manipulated by sticks and wires. The birds, fish, rabbits and kangaroos were manipulated by wires. The wires were heavy enough to be controlled easily. Light-weight wires would bend and sway too readily. When a figure is managed by wires, it is always necessary to keep the figure close against the screen; this makes it easier to control the movements of the figure.

While the group worked, someone often played the records of the "Carnival of the Animals"; thus the music had become familiar to the group long before the play was given. When the screen was at last finished, the ends were fastened to two wood rolls; these in turn were fastened to the frame. One photograph shows the rolls, ratchets and handles. The other shows the screen and frame in use.

At last the day came when the screen and animals were completed. Everyone was excited and eager for the rehearsals to begin.

Slowly the organization was developed—with every member of the group feeling the full importance of even the smallest duty. One slight slip or mark of carelessness would spoil the perfection of the play. The unrolling of the screen was handled with precision and care, a difficult task. Those who sat in front of the screen during rehearsals were alert and quick to see where the screen might be improved. They were generous, and thoughtless of themselves, their whole interest being to give a beautiful shadow play.

During one of the rehearsals someone suggested that the scene for the march of the lions would be more effective if the screen were flooded with a yellow-orange light—to suggest the heat of a tropical country.

Then someone else said the aquarium should have a blue-green atmosphere. Finally a strip of glass about twenty inches long, and narrow enough to pass before the lens, was painted with Japanese water colors—a yellow section for the first scene, blue and blue-green for the second scene, and so on. The colors were not intense, but added to the general effect of a scene.

It would be possible to paint the scenes for this play on glass instead of on the screen. In that case you would have a screen three by five feet, and project the scenery onto the screen from the lantern slide.

When the play was given at the Cleveland Museum of Art, and later in Severance Hall, everything moved smoothly and in perfect harmony with the music. It was a rare and satisfying experience for the entire group, and if Camille Saint-Saëns could have seen the pleasure his "Carnival of the Animals" gave to hundreds of children, he would no doubt have been greatly pleased.

# PART III

# Human Shadow Plays

Scenes from "The Indian and the Oki"

Action scenes from "The Indian and the Oki"

## CHAPTER V

# Making a Human Shadow Play

WHAT IS a human shadow play? Did you ever as a small child dance in the sunlight for the fun of seeing your shadow dance, too? Have you played shadow games using your fingers and hands for casting shadows on a wall? Have you hung a sheet in a doorway and used a light some distance behind you to cast your shadow on the sheet for those on the other side of the sheet to guess your identity? If you have engaged in any one of these forms of amusement, you have actually given a simple shadow play.

What would the world be like without shadows? Shadows of trees in summer upon the grass! Shadows of winter trees upon a wall! Shadows of a vine against a window shade! How much less beauty there would be in the world if there were no shadows. Mankind has always felt the fascination of shadows from earliest times. Once a Persian poet wrote:

*We are no other than a moving row*
*Of magic shadow shapes that come and go.*

If you were going to create a shadow world of your own with yourselves making the shadows upon the screen, what kind of a story would you use for this human shadow play? Is the field of choice as wide as that for the cut-out shadow play? Perhaps not, but it is wide enough to give you an opportunity to use some of the Bible stories, folk tales, ballads, legends and hero tales, also historical incidents.

After choosing your subject, or the story for your play, gather together everything that will make the subject more vivid to you. For instance, if you have chosen a historical incident, you will need to study the people of the time, their manners, customs and dress. These are the qualities that will give atmosphere to your play.

You will enjoy writing for human shadows as much as you did for cut-out shadows if you know your subject well and keep the limitations in mind.

The characters do not speak their lines, which means that you need not follow the formal play structure; you can use the narrative form. Either one or two readers tell the story as the scene is being played, or between the scenes. Music is usually needed, and adds a great deal to the human shadow play.

The screen for this type of shadow play must of necessity be large. A fine quality of sheeting ninety inches wide is excellent. By using the width for the height of the screen, and making the length twelve feet, you will have a screen of good proportions.

The frame should be of wood about two and a half or three inches wide, hinged in the middle of the long sides to make storing more convenient when not in use. The sheeting is stretched taut upon the frame, the tacks about two inches apart. The stretching requires a certain amount of skill in handling, but a well-stretched screen makes for clear-cut shadows.

Scenery and properties for this large screen are made of beaver board, three-ply wood or, in some cases, of heavy cardboard. Light-weight bristol board or oak tag construction paper can be used for making grass, flowers, leaves and fruit. Straw or raffia can be used successfully to suggest a thatched roof or shelter.

Always keep in mind that a true artist suggests with few characteristic lines much more than a poor artist will tell with a mass of useless detail.

Begin to plan your scenery by making a sketch of the scene as a whole upon a large sheet of unprinted newspaper. Block in the silhouette with charcoal or black show-card color or crayons. Try to express a great deal with the fewest possible lines. Remember that you need a great deal of space for the shadows of the figures, so do not crowd your scene.

Now let us imagine that a large rock plays an important part in a scene. You can suggest its size by showing little of the rock and by placing it at the extreme edge of the screen. If it is to be a shelter for a figure, it must be higher than the figure. Make it overhanging, make it seem to protect one who would stand against it. If a figure is to climb the rock make the contour suggest a rock that could be climbed. Now is the rock to have a sharp, jagged contour, or is it to be softened by grasses and flowering plants that grow out from the crevice and in the hollows?

If you need a tree, decide on the kind and then simplify your drawing, keeping the main characteristics in mind. If it leans as though blown by the wind, take care that the grasses and plants at its roots lean in the same direction.

When you have the scenery and properties made, you are ready to think of lighting. A 400-watt bulb will give you a strong light, casting clear-cut shadows. You may wish to use color. This is possible by using Japanese water colors on glass. You will have to use some glue with the water colors to make them adhere to the glass. You can paint distant hills, trees and sky very effectively, and project the color onto the screen by placing the glass before the light. Sheets of colored gelatin are sometimes used; however, the color is usually quite intense. Why not experiment with cellophane? Lighting your play is a very interesting and worth-while problem, and goes a long way in helping you to make a beautiful play. The lighting of the scene should always harmonize with the mood of the scene. A rheostat or dimmer to control your light is almost a necessity. The drawing opposite gives you directions for making a dimmer in your workshop.

New problems will constantly confront you that are a challenge to your dramatic ability and imagination. In making the cut-out shadow figure you have the silhouette before you to criticize, change and improve. You are the spectator as well as the creator. But in the human shadow play, you yourself are the shadow figure. You must use your imagination and the suggestions given you by the director if you wish to create a silhouette that is in character with the part you are playing.

It will not be enough for you to wish to portray a certain character; you must have the form, the height and the profile that will suggest the character as well as the dramatic skill to act as the character would act.

Although you do not speak for the character you are to portray, you will soon realize that your actions are as expressive as words would be. Surprise, excitement, joy, sadness, discouragement, dignity, anger,

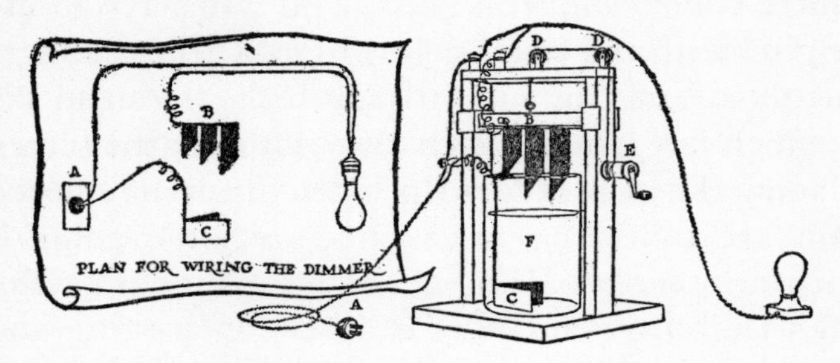


From *a* the current from one wire passes to the stationary electrode *c* which is submerged in a gallon jar of water containing one eighth teaspoon of ammonium chloride. The graduated electrodes (all connected) are fastened to the wooden bar *b* which is made to slide up and down the vertical posts at either side. Both sets of electrodes are made of thin sheet copper. By means of the cord (attached to the screw eye in *b*) which runs over the pulleys *d, d* down to the spool drum *e,* the upper electrodes can be slowly let down into the ammonium chloride solution, completing the circuit and increasing it as more of the electrode surface is exposed to the liquid.

fright, tenderness and many more emotions can be expressed through pantomime quite as clearly as by the voice. Pantomime is a very old art. The Greek actor of ancient times depended largely upon pantomime to carry his message to his audience. In the fifteenth and sixteenth centuries the actors of the *commedia dell'arte* delighted the people of town and country with their expressive and amusing pantomimic skill.

You will find that practice and more practice is

needed to acquire characteristic posture and actions. Suppose you wish to show sadness. A slightly drooping head might convey the mood, but if discouragement is to be expressed, let the shoulders droop as well as the head, to suggest a feeling of sagging muscles, of tired mind and body.

First analyze the character you are about to portray, then his actions under the various conditions in the play. Then study and practice each action until your shadow conveys to the group what you have in mind.

Costuming the character calls for inventiveness and imagination, too. The silhouette is all-important, and more likely than not the costume that looks exactly right in front of the screen will look quite a different thing as a shadow upon the screen.

A figure can be very nice indeed, as far as color goes, but might be a very dumpy and uninteresting shadow. Never cease experimenting until you find just the thing you need to make the silhouette what you wish it to be.

The success of the play depends upon a fine spirit of co-operation and selflessness. "The play's the thing." Therefore you are only important in so far as you contribute to the success of the play.

If your group desire to create a beautiful shadow play, and work whole-heartedly toward that end, you cannot fail. Whatever you do will have elements of beauty and dramatic interest.

## A Group of Human Shadow Plays

THE INDIAN AND THE OKI
THE SHEPHERDESS AND THE PRINCE
THE NATIVITY

## THE INDIAN AND THE OKI

Suggestions for presenting E. Templeton Mitchell's "The Indian and the Oki" which may serve as suggestions for other human shadow plays.

The reason for choosing "The Indian and the Oki" for a human shadow play was that it had action and characters that were very individual, such as would be easily recognized when they fell on the shadow screen. Another reason for choosing this story was that its scenery could be suggested by silhouettes. The group of boys and girls who gave this play selected important incidents of the story and rearranged them and added incidents wherever they found it necessary. The following twelve incidents made up the first act.

INCIDENT I—Rabbit wiggles ears, hops across stage.

INCIDENT II—Sparrows scrap upon rock, first gently, growing furious.

INCIDENT III—Eagle swoops across and down upon rock; birds leave.

INCIDENT IV—Wildcat moves slightly, winks eye, raises tail, arches back ready for spring as

INCIDENT V—Scandawatti peeps from rock, then disappears; then Indian lad appears; with bow and arrow and shoots at wildcat, hits bear.

INCIDENT VI—Bear bounds forward, pulls out arrow from shoulder with teeth, eyes flash, rushes forward as lad attempts to climb rock, misses hold at top, slips, almost falls backward, bear ready to pounce.

INCIDENT VII—Achilles appears at right side, shoots quickly. Bear rolls over, Scandawatti leaps to feet, looks in surprise from bear to Achilles, comes forward, examines gun.

INCIDENT VIII—Chief enters from right slowly, approaches boys. Lad tells him of escape.

INCIDENT IX—French trapper enters from left, approaches, lays hand on Achilles, hears story. Scandawatti leads way to Chief Illiol. Trapper gives pistols to both boys, who admire them. Chief nods satisfaction. Both trapper and chief leave together to right.

INCIDENT X—Boys examine, admire and handle pistols.

INCIDENT XI—Red Deer sneaks from behind rock and looks jealously at weapons, moves hand and body as if eager to possess prize, disappears.

INCIDENT XII—Scene closes as lads pledge friendship and prepare to leave.

The incidents chosen for the second act were:

INCIDENT I—Squaw stirs stew in the kettle that hangs over the fire.

INCIDENT II—Trapper and Chief Illiol enter and sit down. Squaw brings the pipe of peace. They smoke.

INCIDENT III—An Indian enters and dances to the tomtoms. The trapper, chief and dancer leave.

INCIDENT IV—Scandawatti enters with a basket full of fish and Achilles with a game bag full of rabbits and ducks. They give these to the squaw.

INCIDENT V—Scandawatti and Achilles sit on the ground and play with their pistols.
INCIDENT VI—Red Deer peers from behind the bushes.
INCIDENT VII—Squaw gives each boy a bowl of the stew. They eat greedily.
INCIDENT VIII—Boys undo bundle in which there are knives and beads. Achilles holds up the Oki, or false face.
INCIDENT IX—Scandawatti, alarmed, jumps up and runs. Achilles runs after him, carrying the Oki.
INCIDENT X—Red Deer enters stealthily and reaches for the pistols.
INCIDENT XI—Achilles lifts up the Oki from behind a rock. Red Deer drops the pistols and flees.
INCIDENT XII—Scandawatti and Achilles enter laughing, pick up weapons, wrap themselves in blankets and lie down to sleep.

For the third act they chose the following:

INCIDENT I—A turkey runs across the screen.
INCIDENT II—Red Deer follows with Scandawatti. He binds him to a tree, then runs after the turkey.
INCIDENT III—Red Deer returns with dead turkey. Builds a fire and places the turkey over it.
INCIDENT IV—Red Deer dances about, mocking Scandawatti.
INCIDENT V—Achilles peeks from behind rock. Motions to Scandawatti to have courage. Then sticks up the Oki and waves it about in the air.
INCIDENT VI—Red Deer flies in terror.
INCIDENT VII—Achilles frees Scandawatti.

INCIDENT VIII—They devour the turkey.
INCIDENT IX—The trapper and Indian chief appear, and all rejoice.

Shadow plays require just as careful character analysis as any other kind of play. Here is the character analysis.

SCANDAWATTI, *brave, loyal, fun loving.*
ACHILLES, *courageous, loyal, resourceful.*
RED DEER, *treacherous and superstitious.*
CHIEF ILLIOL, *trustworthy and dignified.*
SQUAW, *stolid and good-natured.*
TRAPPER, *just and reliable.*
DANCER, *lively.*

The story included the bear and turkey. The rabbit, wildcat, hawk and birds were added for the sake of the picture. The illustrations show how the turkey, wildcat and birds were made.

The scenery consisted of tree trunks, branches and a big rock cut from beaver board, and foliage, flowers and grasses cut from light-weight bristol board.

The properties needed were a tripod and a kettle, a stick for the fire, a basket of corn, bowls and ladle, pistols, strings of beads, a game bag filled with paper game, a fish basket filled with paper fish, bow and arrow, gun, rope, two blankets and a peace pipe.

The costuming of a shadow play is quite a different problem from the costuming of any other kind of play. A costume may look quite right to the eye and yet be ineffective as a shadow. It requires ingenuity and much experimenting to produce satisfactory silhouettes. Scandawatti, Red Deer and the dancer wore loin cloths, head bands and feathers. The Indian chief wore headdress and blanket. The squaw wore a fringed curtain, head band and beads. The trapper and Achilles wore trappers' costumes and coon-skin caps. A boy took the part of the bear in a bear costume made from outing flannel.

The profiles of the children were not in the least Indian-like. It was necessary to provide them with characteristic noses, and this was done by glueing on flat cut-out paper noses.

The producing of a shadow play requires a director and two assistants, as well as the group of actors. The director is responsible for the production of the play, which will probably require five or six rehearsals. During the first rehearsal he stays behind the screen, working out with the group each incident of the play. He and the group decide upon the entrances, positions on the bridge, the exits, and those who are to manipulate the shadow animals receive their instructions. The reader should be present at the first rehearsal, in order to observe the development of the play. At this rehearsal the actors need not be in costume. Each actor begins by interpreting his part as he feels it should be done. The director should inspire and encourage his actors to do their best, and guard against being too critical at this time, since everyone is feeling his way, becoming familiar with properties and with this new kind of acting in one plane.

It was in the first rehearsal of "The Indian and the Oki" that the boy who took the part of Scandawatti discovered, as he was trying to escape from the bear, that it would look more natural if he got out of the bear's reach by climbing the rock, rather than by dodging behind it. When a stepladder was placed behind the beaver-board rock, the boy, after much practice, was able to make it appear to the audience that he was really climbing the rock. He was finally able to give a little slip as he reached the top, just as the bear was about to overtake him. This gave a real thrill to the young spectators.

At the second rehearsal the director takes his position in front of the screen. He watches every movement and gesture of the actors. He guides the actors, who cannot see their shadows, because they are so close to the screen. If he understands pattern and rhythm, he can direct their movements so that every movement of the shadow play will be beautiful. The reader begins his part at the second rehearsal. He can give an introduction and carry the story on between the acts, or he can read as the play is being given. The reader may be a girl or a boy, and should be chosen for a rich, well-modulated voice, dramatic sense, and ability to enunciate distinctly. The reader should be appropriately costumed.

Introducing a dancer in a shadow play presents a problem. In the second scene of "The Indian and the Oki" you can see in the illustration how the height and bulk and dignity of the Indian chief on the left, and the curved line of the trapper's body on the right, were used to frame the space for the rhythmic movements of the dancer. The dancer also had his problems. The first was that of keeping a characteristic Indian silhouette on the screen at all times. The second problem was that of varying his movements to show his veneration for his chief and his adoration for the Great Spirit. The beating of the tomtom gave the tempo for the steps of his dance. A teacher who understood folk dancing coached the boy who took this part outside of the regular rehearsals, so that he might gain confidence and skill.

By the fourth or fifth rehearsal, if the actors can interpret their parts naturally and convincingly, they will be ready to put on their costumes. Here many surprises await them. As an illustration of this the shepherdess in the play by that name made for herself a very correct little bodice. When she appeared on the shadow screen, her silhouette was very disappointing. In order to give the right effect, a short length of cheesecloth was slashed six or seven times at the ends and then drawn tightly around her, and the slashed ends were tied together down the front. You can see her in the illustration as she kneels on the bridge, manipulating one of the fighting sparrows in the first scene of "The Indian and the Oki." The long heavy braids of this shepherdess were made of yarn.

## THE SHEPHERDESS AND THE PRINCE

The human shadow play "The Shepherdess and the Prince" is a slight, romantic, humorous tale in three scenes, which a group of ninth-grade boys and girls planned, to follow "The Indian and the Oki." A reader told the story as the shadow play was being given. A sketch of the story is as follows.

In the first scene a shepherdess comes in with her sheep. One hand is full of flowers, the other carries her shepherd's crook. She sits down on a grassy hummock and begins to weave a daisy chain, as a folk song is sung off stage, and her sheep nibble at the grass and flowers growing around her. Her pet sheep lays its head affectionately on her knee; she puts the daisy chain around its neck, and, picking a flower, pulls off the petals one by one: he loves me, he loves me not.

A young hunter comes with his game bag on his shoulder. One look at the pretty shepherdess, and he offers his heart straightway. The shepherdess accepts him, and he kisses her hand and promises to return.

The terrible robber baron now enters. He, too, falls in love with the shepherdess, and, opening his game bag, offers her one queer animal after another—long-legged birds, some short-legged and long-necked, a curious assortment. The shepherdess refuses his gifts. He then offers the chain from around his neck, and his heavy purse of gold, but the maiden will have none of him. Enraged, he grabs her by the wrist and drags her to his castle.

The next scene shows the shepherdess weeping as she leans from the tower window, the tops of trees below her. A sad, mournful song is sung off stage. She hears a hunter's call from below. She looks down and then lets down her long braids of hair by which the young prince manages to climb the last few feet of the tower. They plan to escape. A rope ladder is tied to the window, and they let themselves down. Then a shout from without, and the robber baron comes to the window brandishing a long spear and shaking his fists in anger.

The next scene is in a meadow or woodland. A friar is gathering herbs. The prince and the shepherdess come in hand in hand. The prince tells the friar his true name and asks the holy man to marry them. They sink to their knees, and the friar raises his hands in blessing.

The photographs show the simple settings. The boys and girls made this romantic tale into something very humorous and charming.

## THE NATIVITY

*A Religious Shadow Play and How It Was Produced*

Many beautiful shadow plays can be adapted from heroic and religious literature, especially from the Bible. Music can be used with such plays and is especially appropriate for plays celebrating Christmas and Easter.

"The First Christmas," a human shadow play given at the Cleveland Museum of Art, combined music and drama and proved interesting to both children and adults. Some details of the production of this play are offered here in the hope that they may suggest possibilities for similar celebrations in schools and churches. This play grew out of a wish to learn the possibilities of human actors in impressive religious roles, performing behind the shadow screen, also out of a belief that here was a relatively new field of dramatic art. The first step was a careful reading and re-reading of the Prophets and the Gospel, noting those passages which seemed to give the story of the Christ Child in such a way that it could be visually represented on the shadow screen. The following five scenes were finally selected:

SCENE I—The Prophecies
SCENE II—The Annunciation
SCENE III—The Journey to Jerusalem
SCENE IV—The Shepherd
SCENE V—The Adoration

A group of ninth-grade boys and girls from the near-by Fairmount Junior High Training School, with the consent of their principal and teachers, were eager to undertake the two required performances to be given in the auditorium of the Art Museum. The Department of Musical Art of the Art Museum volunteered to share the responsibility for the musical program with Fairmount Junior High School's Department of Music.

The next step was to explain clearly and in detail the plan for the entire program to the young people who were to perform the play. There were characters to be studied and interpreted so that they would suggest biblical traditions. There were also costumes and properties to be planned, which must also be traditional. Since there were no lines to be spoken by these characters, the important requirement was ability to realize a character and to interpret it through pantomime. Pantomime is a very exacting art, and it was soon found that some members of the group had little or no ability in this field, while others could interpret character with little effort. The shadow screen was used when parts were being assigned. For example, it was necessary to have a slender young girl with delicate features for the role of the Madonna, and also for the angel in the scene of the annunciation. Stature was considered, for the difference in the heights of the actors gave interest and individuality to a scene. The faces of the young boys were in some cases strengthened by building out the nose or using a flat cut-out paper nose glued to the actor's nose.

Reference books and plates were carefully studied and drawings made from the illustrations of Tissot and Doré. Finally the size and proportions of the shadow screen must be studied, since each shadow actor must do his part within a very limited space, and that not the usual three-dimensional space, but in a flat two-dimensional space. All the action must be absolutely in silhouette from right to left or left to right. Of course the director of any shadow play, whether cut-out or human, will take advantage of certain accidental effects which may seem at times to contradict the above statement. It may be a turn of the head, shoulder or a hand, or it may be a very fine effect produced when a figure moves even an inch nearer or farther from the shadow screen. The point is that the director and the whole group, with the exception of those performing in each scene, should be as alert and exacting as a movie director if the final results are to be really beautiful. In fact, the producing of a fine shadow play is a triumph for the entire group that undertakes it, for it means that they have understood design and composition with figures that change every moment but always come into interesting and expressive new relations and compositions.

The proscenium of the Cleveland Art Museum stage was entirely too high and wide to be filled with the shadow screen. It was decided to design a shadow screen of suitable proportions for the human actors, using heavy curtains to surround the frame. The center panel had been used previously as a screen for the human shadow play, "The Indian and the Oki." This was now turned upright, and side panels were fastened to it with hinges. Pointed arches were designed on heavy paper; these were cut out and attached to the top and inside of the shadow screen. These arches at once suggested a Gothic church setting. For the Adoration scene a rude shelter was built within which the Madonna might sit as she held the Christ Child (photograph).

The properties for the five scenes were as follows:

SCENE I—The Prophecies

Two staffs and a large book.

SCENE II—The Annunciation

Angel's wings, halo, and scepter, seat for Madonna.

SCENE III—The Journey to Bethlehem.

The entrance porch to the inn, the rock, Joseph's staff, the inn keeper's keys.

SCENE IV—The Shepherds

The shepherds' staffs, two sheep, one lamb, a long narrow piece of beaver board, the contour of which suggested distant mountains. (This was placed a foot or so from the screen, which made the shadow lighter and suggested distance.) A strip of grasses and flowers.

SCENE V—The Adoration

The shelter for the Madonna mentioned before, the crowns and gifts of the Wise Men, the halos for Madonna and Christ Child.

*Costuming the Nativity Play:* The usual problems of costuming could be dismissed in this play, since neither materials nor colors were important, not being seen by the audience. But the silhouettes of the characters were very important. It was found that cheesecloth served many purposes. You can see the effect it produces when wrapped about the heads of the shepherds. It was used for head coverings and to build out figures. Bathrobes were used for the shepherds' costumes. Suggestions for these properties were found in early Italian paintings, especially in those of Fra Angelico.

The designs for the halos were traced on oiled stencil board. A light-weight stiff cardboard would do as well. Then certain parts were cut away and the openings covered with a piece of yellow gelatine. The wings were made of stiff cardboard, the design of the feathers cut out, and colored gelatine used to cover the opening. The wings were tied about the shoulders and waist of the character taking the part of the angel. The halos were tied about the heads of the young girls taking the part of the Madonna and the angel, and the large doll which was used for the Christ Child. The photograph will show you the halos, wings and scepter used in the second scene.

The sheep used in the fourth scene were cut from heavy cardboard and attached to narrow wooden platforms for the purpose of holding them upright. The heads of the large sheep were movable and managed by a wire. The slightest movement of the head made them seem alive. The photograph shows two of the sheep and a strip of flowers and grasses.

*Lighting Effects:* Just as the costumes and acting must suggest the scene, so must the lighting effects suggest and heighten the mood of the scene and, taken together, must carry on the whole dramatic movement. Naturally, each scene required appropriate lighting.

For example: Scene I seemed to require a certain mixture of blue and purple to suggest the far-off days of the Prophets. Scene II, the Annunciation, required a warmer and more personal kind of lighting, so a lemon-yellow was used. In Scene III a bluish light suggested the starlight in which the journey to Bethlehem was made. Scene IV, a deeper blue light for the shepherds guarding their flocks at night. Scene V, The Adoration, required warm, glowing, golden light. For each of these scenes ordinary colored gelatine proved disappointing. After many experiments and failures, it was found that the finest effects could be produced by painting colors for each scene onto a large piece of glass that would pass before the clear glass of the lantern. This glass was painted with a solution of Japanese water colors, such as are used in coloring lantern slides, LePage's glue and water. Greater intensity of color could be obtained by repainting when the first coat was dry. It was also possible to suggest scenery by this means of painting. In the photographs of the Adoration you can see how the painting suggests deep space in the golden light in the center, as it surrounds the Virgin and grows darker toward the edges of the frame. The glass used for the Nativity was twelve by twenty-four inches. The edges of the glass were bound with adhesive tape to insure safety. An extra carrier for this larger piece of glass was made and attached to the lantern. As the center panel of the shadow screen was twelve feet high by seven and a half feet wide, and the side panels were ten feet high and four and a quarter feet wide it was necessary to flood the entire screen with colored light. As a safety precaution a piece of asbestos was placed under the lantern, and another piece was used with an opening which allowed the light to fully flood the screen but not pass beyond. The lantern was placed eight to ten feet behind the shadow screen, which was all the distance possible. More space is highly desirable for so large a screen. A 400-watt light was used.

*The Reader:* An experienced reader with a rich, well-modulated voice contributed much to the success of the play by his understanding of the dramatic and musical requirements.

*Rehearsals:* There were very few rehearsals, but these were always carried on with the reader, who in a sense led the action. Entrances and exits were timed to the reading. The operator of the lights also took his cue from the reader. Music added greatly to the feeling of reverence "The Nativity" inspired. The Fairmount choir sang the carols for two of the four performances. These carols were sung between the scenes without a musical accompaniment. A young girl with a full sweet voice sang "Here Where the Rose and Lily Bloom" in the scene of the Adoration after the reader in the scene had ceased speaking. The lights on the scene were slowly extinguished as she sang the closing lines. "Silent Night" was sung by the choir as they left the auditorium. They wore the surplice or cape of the traditional choir boy, and during the play were seated close to the right of the stage, against a bank of Christmas trees.

At the final performances for the public there was neither break nor hesitation. The reading, acting, lighting and music seemed to have a unity and a flow that was simple and beautiful, moving and reverent, and to carry something of the age-old mystery of the shadow.

## THE NATIVITY

*A Shadow Play Given by Fairmount Junior High Training School and the Saturday Morning Music Classes of the Cleveland Museum of Art*

### PROGRAM

PROCESSIONAL

Bring a Torch, Jeanette, Isabelle
French Carol

From Far Away — Traditional Carol

SCENE I THE PROPHECIES

Lo, How a Rose E'er Blooming
Michael Praetorius 1571–1621

SCENE II THE ANNUNCIATION

Oh, Little Town of Bethlehem
Lewis R. Redner

SCENE III THE JOURNEY TO BETHLEHEM

Shepherds, Shake Off Your Drowsy Sleep
Besacon Carol

SCENE IV THE ANGEL AND THE SHEPHERDS

I Know, O Virgin Mary
French Carol

SCENE V THE ADORATION

Here Where the Rose and Lily Bloom
François Gevaert 1828–1908

RECESSIONAL

Silent Night — Franz Graber

"The Shepherdess and the Prince," a human shadow play

*Scene* I

*Scene* II

*Scene* III

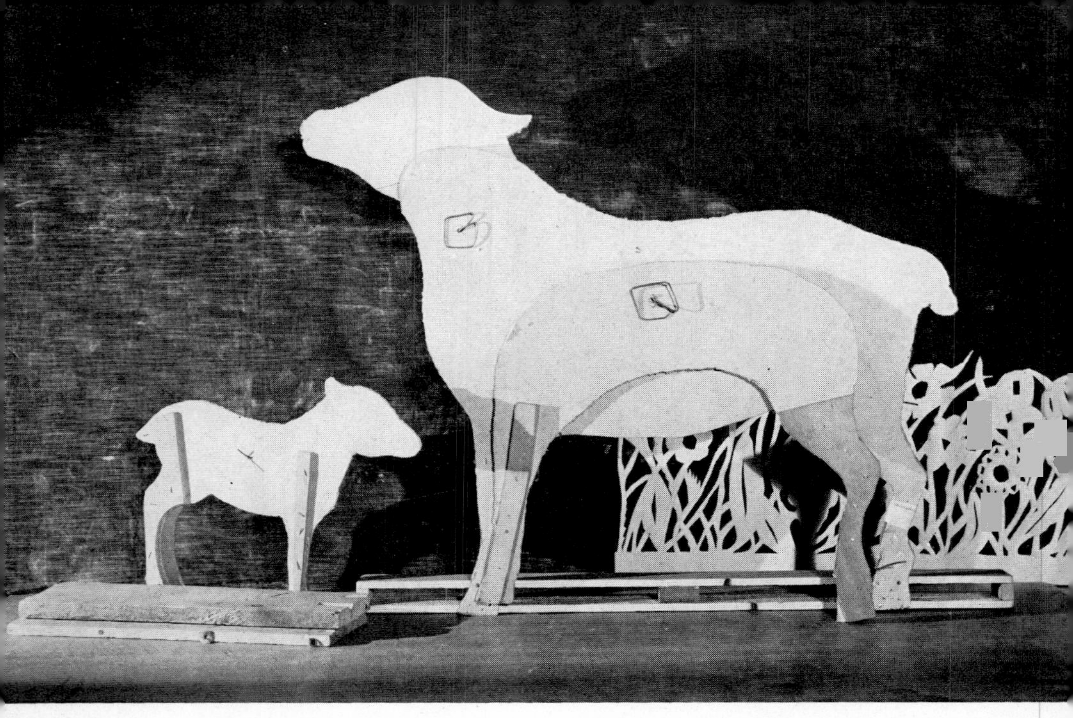

Animal cut-outs used in "The First Christmas"

Properties used in "The First Christmas"

## HUMAN SHADOW PLAYS

### SCENE I

*The Prophecies*

The prophet ISAIAH speaks:

"And thus spake the prophet ISAIAH:

"And it shall come to pass in the last days, that the mountain of the Lord's house shall be established in the top of the mountains, and shall be exalted above the hills; and all nations shall flow unto it.

"And many people shall go and say, Come ye, and let us go up to the mountain of the Lord, to the house of the God of Jacob; and he will teach us of his ways, and we will walk in his paths: for out of Zion shall go forth the law, and the word of the Lord from Jerusalem.

"And he shall judge among the nations, and shall rebuke many people: and they shall beat their swords into plowshares, and their spears into pruninghooks: . . ."

"Behold, a king shall reign in righteousness, and princes shall rule in judgment."

(*Isaiah 32:1*)

"Therefore the Lord himself shall give you a sign; Behold, a virgin shall conceive, and bear a son, and shall call his name Immanuel."

(*Isaiah 7:14*)

"For unto us a child is born, unto us a son is given: and the government shall be upon his shoulder: and his name shall be called Wonderful, Counsellor, The mighty God, The everlasting Father, The Prince of Peace."

(*Isaiah 9:6*)

The prophet MALACHI speaks:

"And thus spake the prophet MALACHI:

"Behold, I will send my messenger, and he shall prepare the way before me: and the Lord, whom ye seek, shall suddenly come to his temple, even the messenger of the covenant, whom ye delight in: behold, he shall come, saith the Lord of hosts.

"But who may abide the day of his coming? and who shall stand when he appeareth? for he is like a refiner's fire. . . .

"And he shall sit as a refiner and purifier of silver: and he shall purify the sons of Levi, and purge them as gold and silver, that they may offer unto the Lord an offering in righteousness.

"Then shall the offering of Judah and Jerusalem be pleasant unto the Lord as in the days of old, and as in former years."

(*Malachi 3:1–4*)

"For, behold, the day cometh, that shall burn as an oven; and all the proud, yea, and all that do wickedly, shall be stubble: and the day that cometh shall burn them up, saith the Lord of hosts, that it shall leave them neither root nor branch.

"But unto you that fear my name shall the Sun of righteousness arise with healing in his wings, and ye shall go forth, and grow up as calves of the stall. . . .

"And he shall turn the heart of the fathers to the children, and the heart of the children to their fathers. . . ."

(*Malachi 4:1,2,6*)

The prophet MICAH speaks:

"And thus spake the prophet MICAH:

"But thou, Bethlehem Ephratah, though thou be little among the thousands of Judah, yet out of thee shall he come forth unto me that is to be ruler in Israel; whose goings forth have been from old, from everlasting. . . ."

(*Micah 5:2*)

"And he shall stand and feed in the strength of the Lord, in the majesty of the name of the Lord his God; and they shall abide: for now shall he be great unto the ends of the earth."

(*Micah 5:2, 4*)

"He hath shewed thee, O man, what is good; and what doth he require of thee, but to do justly, and to love mercy, and to walk humbly with thy God?"

(*Micah 6:8*)

"And many nations shall come, and say, Come, and let us go up to the mountain of the Lord, and to the house of the God of Jacob; and he will teach us of his ways. . . .

"And he shall judge among many people, and rebuke strong nations afar off; and they shall beat their swords into plowshares and their spears into pruning hooks: nation shall not lift up a sword against nation, neither shall they learn war any more. . . .

"For all people will walk every one in the name of his God and we will walk in the name of the Lord our God forever and ever."

(*Micah 4:2, 3, 5*)

## SCENE II

### *The Annunciation*

"And . . . the angel Gabriel was sent from God unto a city of Galilee, named Nazareth,

"To a virgin espoused to a man whose name was Joseph, of the house of David; and the virgin's name was Mary.

"And the angel came in unto her and said, Hail, thou that art highly favored, the Lord is with thee: blessed art thou among women.

"And when she saw him, she was troubled at his saying, and cast in her mind what manner of salutation this should be.

"And the angel said unto her, Fear not, Mary; for thou hast found favor with God.

"And, behold, thou shalt conceive . . . and bring forth a son, and shalt call his name Jesus.

"He shall be great, and shall be called the Son of the Highest: and the Lord God shall give unto him the throne of his father David:

"And he shall reign over the house of Jacob for ever; and of his kingdom there shall be no end.

"Then said Mary unto the angel, How shall this be? . . .

"And the angel answered and said unto her, The Holy Ghost shall come upon thee, and the power of the Highest shall overshadow thee: therefore also that holy thing which shall be born of thee shall be called the Son of God. . . ."

(*St. Luke 1:26–35*)

"And Mary said, My soul doth magnify the Lord,

"And my spirit hath rejoiced in God my Saviour.

"For he hath regarded the low estate of his handmaiden: for, behold, from henceforth all generations shall call me blessed.

"For he that is mighty hath done to me great things; and holy is his name.

"And his mercy is on them that fear him from generation to generation.

"He hath shewed strength with his arm; he hath scattered the proud in the imagination of their hearts.

"He hath put down the mighty from their seats and exalted them of low degree."

(*St. Luke 1:46–52*)

## SCENE III

### *The Journey to Bethlehem*

"And it came to pass in those days, that there went out a decree from Caesar Augustus, that all the world should be taxed.

"(And this taxing was first made when Cyrenius was governor of Syria.)

"And all went to be taxed, every one into his own city.

"And Joseph also went up from Galilee, out of the city of Nazareth, into Judea, unto the city of David, which is called Bethlehem; (because he was of the house and lineage of David:)

"To be taxed with Mary his espoused wife. . . ."

(*St. Luke 2:1–5*)

## SCENE IV

### *The Angel and the Shepherds*

"And there were in the same country shepherds abiding in the field, keeping watch over their flock by night.

"And lo, the angel of the Lord came upon them, and the glory of the Lord shone round about them: and they were sore afraid.

"And the angel said unto them, Fear not: for, behold, I bring you good tidings of great joy, which shall be to all people.

"For unto you is born this day in the city of David a Saviour, which is Christ the Lord.

"And this shall be a sign unto you; Ye shall find the babe wrapped in swaddling clothes, lying in a manger.

"And suddenly there was with the angel a multitude of the heavenly host praising God, and saying,

"Glory to God in the highest, and on earth peace, good will toward men.

"And it came to pass, as the angels were gone away from them into heaven, the shepherds said one to another, Let us now go even unto Bethlehem, and see this thing which is come to pass, which the Lord has made known unto us."

(*St. Luke 2:8–15*)

## SCENE V

### *The Adoration*

"Now when Jesus was born in Bethlehem of Judaea in the days of Herod the king, behold, there came wise men from the east to Jerusalem,

"Saying, Where is he that is born King of the Jews? for we have seen his star in the east, and are come to worship him. . . .

". . . and, lo, the star, which they saw in the east, went before them, till it came and stood over where the young child was. . . .

"And when they were come into the house, they saw the young child with Mary his mother, and fell down, and worshipped him: and when they had opened their treasures, they presented unto him gifts; gold, and frankincense, and myrrh."

(*Matthew 2:1,2,9,11*)

# A LIST OF BOOKS CONTAINING STORIES FOR ADAPTATION INTO SHADOW PLAYS

"The First Christmas"
*Scene* I, The Prophets.

*Scene* III, The journey to Bethlehem

*Scene* IV, The Angel and the Shepherds

*Scene* V, The Adoration. From the human shadow play, "The First Christmas"

Glasses painted for scenes from "The First Christmas"

A. Glass painted with blue violet water colors for the first scene.

B. An orange-yellow for the scene of the Adoration. The space within the center was not painted.

C. Pale yellow for the scene of the Annunciation.

D. Blue deepening to purple in the mountains for the scene of the shepherds. The space within the circles was not painted. This space suggested the light of the Star of Bethlehem.

A

B

C

D

# A LIST OF BOOKS CONTAINING STORIES FOR ADAPTATION INTO SHADOW PLAYS

## FABLES

| Title | Author | Publisher | Price |
|---|---|---|---|
| *Æsop's Fables, Told Anew and Their History Traced* | Joseph Jacobs | Macmillan | $1.00 |
| *Basket Woman* | Mary Austin | Houghton | $2.00 |
| *Book of Fables and Folk Stories* | Horace E. Scudder | Houghton Mifflin | $1.60 |

Contains most familiar of the fables and folk tales: Little Red Riding Hood; Puss in Boots; Elves and the Shoemaker; Jack and the Beanstalk; Cinderella; Tortoise and the Hare; Sleeping Beauty in the Wood; Dick Whittington and His Cat; Beauty and the Beast; Traveling Musicians of Bremen.

| Title | Author | Publisher | Price |
|---|---|---|---|
| *Fables* | La Fontaine | Dutton | $1.00 |
| *Hindu Fables for Little Children* | Dhan Gopal Mukerji | Dutton | $1.00 |

Contains ten stories about monkeys, cows, rabbits, elephants, and crocodiles. Each story brings out some point of humor, or of wisdom of the East.

| Title | Author | Publisher | Price |
|---|---|---|---|
| *Tortoise and the Geese, and Other Stories* | Bidpai | Houghton | $1.50 |

## FOLKLORE AND FAIRY TALES

| Title | Author | Publisher | Price |
|---|---|---|---|
| *Adventures of Pinocchio* | Carlo Lorenzini | Macmillan | $1.00 |

## SHADOW PLAYS

| Title | Author | Publisher | Price |
|---|---|---|---|
| *Aladdin and the Wonderful Lamp, and Other Stories* | Andrew Lang | Longmans | $1.25 |
| *Alice's Adventures in Wonderland and Through the Looking Glass* . . . . . . . | Lewis Carroll | Macmillan | $1.00 |
| *Arabian Nights' Entertainment* . . . . . . | E. W. Lane | Holt | $2.00 |
| Includes the following stories: Fisherman and the Genie; Magic Horse; Seven Voyages of Sinbad of the Sea; Caliph the Fisherman; Ali Baba and the Forty Thieves; Aladdin and the Wonderful Lamp. | | | |
| *A Roundabout Turn* . . . . . . . . . . | Robert H. Charles | Warne & Co. | $1.50 |
| *Atlantic Treasury of Childhood Stories* . . . . | Mary D. K. Hodgkins | Little Brown | $2.50 |
| *East o' the Sun and West o' the Moon* . . . . | Mrs. Gudrun Thorne-Thomsen | Row Peterson | $ .68 |
| Twenty-two Norwegian folk tales. | | | |
| *English Fairy Tales* . . . . . . . . . . | Joseph Jacobs | Putnam | $1.75 |
| Includes: Jack and the Beanstalk; Johnny-Cake; Jack the Giant Killer; Whittington and His Cat; and about twenty-five other tales. | | | |
| *Fairy Book* . . . . . . . . . . . . . . | Dinah M. Craik | Macmillan | $2.50 |
| Includes: Snowwhite and Rosered; Bremen Town Musicians; Frog Prince; Six Swans; Rumpelstilzken; and other stories. | | | |
| *Hans Christian Andersen Fairy Tales* . . . . | Mrs. Edgar Lucas | Dutton | $2.00 |
| *Iván the Fool and Other Tales* . . . . . . | Count Leo Tolstoi | Oxford | $1.75 |
| *Japanese Fairy Tales* . . . . . . . . . . | William E. Griffis | Crowell | $1.75 |

## STORIES FOR SHADOW PLAYS

| Title | Author | Publisher | Price |
|---|---|---|---|
| *Johnny-Cake* | Joseph Jacobs | Putnam | $1.00 |
| *Jungle Book* | Rudyard Kipling | Doubleday | $2.50 |
| *Just So Stories* | Rudyard Kipling | Doubleday | $2.50 |
| How the Elephant Got His Trunk and other stories. | | | |
| *Nights with Uncle Remus* | Joel Chandler Harris | Houghton Mifflin | $2.50 |
| Includes: Brer Fox; Brer Rabbit; Tar Baby; and other tales. | | | |
| *Old Ballads in Prose* | Eva M. Tappan | Houghton Mifflin | $1.75 |
| Saddle to Rags; Barring of the Door; and other tales. | | | |
| *Peter and Wendy* | Sir James M. Barrie | Scribners | $2.50 |
| How Wendy, John and Michael flew with Peter Pan to the Never-never-land. Adventures with pirates, redskins and the fairy Tinker Bell. | | | |
| *Picture Folk Tales* | Valéry Carrick | Stokes | $1.50 |
| *Pied Piper of Hamelin* | Robert Browning | Lippincott | $1.00 |
| *Rip Van Winkle* | Washington Irving | Macmillan | $1.00 |
| *Rose and the Ring* | William Thackeray | Macmillan | $1.00 |
| *Russian Grandmother's Wonder Tales* | Louise Houghton | Scribners | $2.00 |
| *Skazki; Tales and Legends of Old Russia* | Ida Zeitlin | Farrar | $2.00 |

## SHADOW PLAYS

| Title | Author | Publisher | Price |
|---|---|---|---|
| *Sokar and the Crocodile* | Alice W. Howard | Macmillan | $2.00 |
| *Tales from Scottish Ballads* | Elizabeth W. Grierson | Macmillan | $1.75 |
| *The Cat Who Went to Heaven* | Elizabeth J. Coatsworth | Macmillan | $2.00 |
| *Water-Babies* | Charles Kingsley | Houghton | $2.00 |
| *Whins on Knockattan* | Anne T. Casserley | Harper | $1.50 |
| *Wind in the Willows* | Kenneth Grahame | Scribners | $1.00 |

## HEROES, MYTHS AND LEGENDS

| Title | Author | Publisher | Price |
|---|---|---|---|
| *Abe Lincoln Grows Up* | Carl Sandburg | Harcourt | $2.50 |
| *Adventures of Odysseus* | Padraic Colum | Macmillan | $2.00 |
| *Æneid for Boys and Girls* | Alfred John Church | Macmillan | $2.00 |
| *American History Stories for Young Readers* | Eva M. Tappan | Houghton | $1.75 |
| *Boy Scouts' Life of Lincoln* | Ida M. Tarbell | Macmillan | $2.00 |
| *Boys' Life of Washington* | Helen Nicolay | Appleton-Century | $2.50 |
| *Children of Odin* | Padraic Colum | Macmillan | $2.50 |
| *Christ Legends* | Selma Lagerlöf | Holt | $1.75 |

## STORIES FOR SHADOW PLAYS

| Title | Author | Publisher | Price |
|---|---|---|---|
| *Courtship of Miles Standish* | Henry W. Longfellow | Houghton | $ .44 |
| *Christmas in Legend and Story* | Smith and Hazeltine | Lothrop | $2.50 |
| *Daniel Boone, Wilderness Scout* | Stewart Edward White | Garden City | $1.00 |
| *Davy Crockett* | Constance Rourke | Harcourt | $2.50 |
| *Don Quixote* | Miguel de Cervantes | Macmillan | $1.00 |
| *Evangeline* | Henry W. Longfellow | Houghton | $ .44 |
| *Famous Men of Greece* | Haaren & A. B. Poland | American Book Co. | $ .72 |
| *Famous Men of Rome* | Haaren & A. B. Poland | American Book Co. | $ .72 |
| *Famous Men of the Middle Ages* | Haaren & A. B. Poland | American Book Co. | $ .72 |
| *Girl in White Armor* | Albert Bigelow Paine | Macmillan | $1.50 |
| *God's Troubadour* | Sophie Jewett | Crowell | $2.00 |
| *Golden Age of Myth and Legend* | T. Bulfinch | Stokes | $4.00 |
| *Golden Porch, A Book of Greek Fairy Tales* | W. M. Hutchinson | Longmans Green | $2.00 |
| *Good Stories for Great Holidays* | Frances Olcott | Houghton | $3.00 |

Little Piccola; The Stranger Child; Saint Christopher; the Christmas Rose; The Wooden Shoes of the Little Wolff; and other tales.

## SHADOW PLAYS

| Title | Author | Publisher | Price |
|---|---|---|---|
| *Gulliver's Travels* | Jonathan Swift | Macmillan | $2.50 |
| *Iliad for Boys and Girls* | Alfred J. Church | Macmillan | $1.75 |
| *In the Days of Alfred the Great* | Eva M. Tappan | Lothrop | $1.50 |
| *Joan of Arc* | Louis Maurice Boutet de Monvel | Appleton | $4.00 |
| *King of the Golden River* | John Ruskin | Macmillan | $1.00 |
| | | Heath | $ .52 |
| *Life in the Greenwood* | Marion F. Lansing | Ginn | $ .64 |
| *Little Brother Francis of Assisi* | Michael Williams | Macmillan | $1.75 |
| *Merry Adventures of Robin Hood* | Howard Pyle | Scribners | $3.00 |
| *Mighty Men from Achilles to Julius Caesar* | Eleanor Farjeon | Appleton-Century | $1.00 |
| *Mighty Men from Beowulf to William the Conqueror* | Eleanor Farjeon | Appleton-Century | $1.00 |
| *Odyssey for Boys and Girls* | Alfred J. Church | Macmillan | $ 1.00 |
| *Page, Esquire, and Knight* | Marion F. Lansing | Ginn | $ .64 |
| *Stories from Old French Romance* | Ethel M. Wilmot-Buxton | Stokes | $1.25 |
| *Stories of Charlemagne and the Twelve Peers of France* | Alfred John Church | Seeley J. S. | 5s. |

## STORIES FOR SHADOW PLAYS

| Title | Author | Publisher | Price |
|---|---|---|---|
| *Stories of Norse Heroes Told by the Northmen* . . | | | |
| | Ethel M. Wilmot-Buxton | Crowell | $2.00 |
| *Story of King Arthur and His Knights* . . . . . | | | |
| | Howard Pyle | Scribners | $3.00 |
| *Story of Sigurd, the Volsung* . . . . . . . | | | |
| | William Morris | Longmans Green | $ .80 |
| *Story of Sir Launcelot and His Companions* . . . | | | |
| | Howard Pyle | Scribners | $3.00 |
| *Story of the Canterbury Pilgrims* . . . . . . | | | |
| | F. J. H. Darton | Stokes | $3.00 |
| *Story of the Champions of the Round Table* . . . | | | |
| | Howard Pyle | Scribners | $3.00 |
| *Tales of Chaucer* . . . . . . . . . . . | | | |
| | Eleanor Farjeon | Hale | $3.00 |
| *Viking Tales* . . . . . . . . . . . . | | | |
| | Jennie Hall | Rand | $ .56 |
| *When Knights Were Bold* . . . . . . . . | | | |
| | Eva M. Tappan | Houghton | $3.00 |

## TALES OF ADVENTURE AND OTHER STORIES

| Title | Author | Publisher | Price |
|---|---|---|---|
| *Adventures of Huckleberry Finn* . . . . . . . | | | |
| | S. L. Clemens | Harper | $2.25 |
| *Adventures of Tom Sawyer* . . . . . . . . | | | |
| | S. L. Clemens | Harper | $2.25 |
| *Black Face—Adventures of a Lamb* . . . . . | | | |
| | Thelma H. Bell | Doubleday, Doran | $1.50 |
| *Heidi* . . . . . . . . . . . . . . | | | |
| | J. H. Spyri | Houghton | $2.00 |
| *Kari, the Elephant* . . . . . . . . . . | | | |
| | Dhan Gopal Mukerji | Dutton | $2.00 |
| *Little Wooden Doll* . . . . . . . . . | | | |
| | Mrs. Margery Bianco | Macmillan | $1.00 |

## SHADOW PLAYS

| Title | Author | Publisher | Price |
|---|---|---|---|
| *Story of Little Black Sambo* | Helen Bannerman | Stokes | $1.50 |
| *The Story of Ferdinand* | Munro Leaf | Viking Press | $1.00 |

## STORIES OF THE BIBLE AND THE SAINTS

| Title | Author | Publisher | Price |
|---|---|---|---|
| *First Bible* | Selected and arranged by J. W. Maury; Illustrated by Helen Sewell | Oxford | $2.50 |
| *In God's Garden* | Amy Steedman | Nelson | $2.00 |

## OPERA

| Title | Author | Publisher | Price |
|---|---|---|---|
| *Story of the Rhinegold* | Anna Alice Chapin | Harper | $2.00 |
| *Wonder Tales from Wagner* | Anna Alice Chapin | Harper | $2.00 |

# BIBLIOGRAPHY AND ACKNOWLEDGMENTS

# BIBLIOGRAPHY

THIS is a very brief bibliography selected from the large number of books and pamphlets that have been written on shadows in many languages through two thousand years. The list of books written in English which include shadows, however, is very short, and includes the following:

*Chinese Shadow Shows,* Genevieve Wimsatt, Harvard University Press, Cambridge, Mass.

*Chinese Shadow-figure Plays and Their Making,* by Benjamin March, Puppetry Imprints.

*Dolls and Puppets,* Max Von Boehn (Trans. by Josephine Nicoll), George G. Harrap and Company, London, England.

*Oriental Theatricals,* Berthold Laufer, Field Museum of Natural History, Chicago, Ill.

*The Book of Marionettes,* Helen Joseph, Viking Press.

*The Home of the Puppet-Play,* Richard Pischel.

*The Golden Bough,* Frazer, Macmillan.

*The Wajang or Shadow Play as Given in Java,* Coos Van Hinloopen Labberton.

*A Book on Chinese Shadows,* in preparation by Pauline Benton.

*History of the Shadow Theater in the East and West,* George Jacob, written in German.

## ACKNOWLEDGMENTS

WE WISH to acknowledge our indebtedness to those who have contributed so much to the making of this book, and to express to them our sincere gratitude. We are indebted to F. Allen Whiting, former director, and William M. Milliken, present director, of The Cleveland Museum of Art, who have considered the shadow play as a legitimate art activity and provided the funds necessary for the Museum's permanent shadow-play equipment. This has made it possible for schools to bring their shadow plays to the Art Museum Saturday afternoons as entertainment for young people.

We are especially indebted to Edd A. Ruggles, photographer and printer of The Cleveland Museum of Art, who made the photographs included in this book which we feel so adequately supplement our text; to Ruth Field Ruggles, in charge of the Museum's lending collection and to other members of the Educational Staff; to Nell G. Sill, the Museum's librarian. Also to John W. McCabe, superintendent of the Art Museum building, and members of his staff for advice and construction of the various types of screens used in presenting the plays included in this book.

Another debt is due Joseph A. Crowell, principal of Fairmount Junior High Training School, and his faculty for co-operation with its Art Department in producing most of the plays included in this book. We extend our sincere thanks to The Cleveland Public Library for many services and courtesies extended us.

We wish to express to Corydon Bell our appreciation of the way in which he has kept the traditional spirit and quality of the Oriental Shadow Makers in his illustrations.

THE AUTHORS

# INDEX

# INDEX